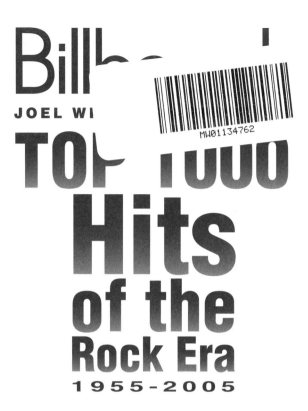

Billboard

JOEL WHITBURN

TOP 1000

Hits
of the
Rock Era
1955-2005

Portions of the *Billboard* chart material in this work were constructed by *Billboard* magazine from information provided by Broadcast Data Systems (BDS), which electronically monitors actual radio airplay, and Soundscan, Inc., which electronically collects Point of Sale information from music retail outlets.

ISBN 1-4234-0919-1

HAL•LEONARD® CORPORATION

7777 W. BLUEMOUND RD. P.O. BOX 13819 MILWAUKEE, WI 53213

Visit Hal Leonard Online at
www.halleonard.com

CONTENTS

JULY 9, 1955 — DECEMBER 24, 2005

Joel Whitburn and Record Research:
The Undisputed Experts on Recorded Music

What began simply as a teenager's record collection nearly 50 years ago has today grown into the largest and most successful business of its kind anywhere in the world.

Joel Whitburn and his Record Research staff have been highlighting the hits, archiving the artists and tracking the trends in recorded music longer, deeper and more definitively than anyone else in the business.

Joel first began collecting records as a teenager growing up in the 1950s. As both his collection and his zeal for record collecting grew through the years, Joel began organizing his records according to the highest positions they reached on *Billboard* magazine's music charts. In 1970, with the encouragement of friends in the music industry, Joel turned his chart-watching hobby into a business with the publication of his first book — a slender volume titled simply *Record Research*.

Over the past 35 years, Joel's company, Record Research Inc., has published 105 reference books, which chronicle well over a century of American music, reaching as far back as 1890. Record Research publications cover virtually every charted music genre, including Pop, Rock, Country, R&B/Hip-Hop, Adult Contemporary, Dance/Disco and more.

These volumes, as well as Joel's books published by Billboard Books, are required reading for virtually anyone with a serious interest in music. Joel has also collaborated with Rhino Records on a series of 150 *Billboard* CD compilations of America's top-charted hits. His own comprehensive charted music collection is the backbone of his research.

≈≈≈

Special thanks to my Record Research staff: Kim Bloxdorf, Brent Olynick, Jeanne Olynick and Paul Haney.

AUTHOR'S NOTE

Welcome to our seventh edition of *Top 1000 Hits*. Readers of earlier editions will notice that we've added the tagline "of the Rock Era" to the title and also see a burst on the front cover stating "50 Years." That's a long time when you consider the many forecasts that rock and roll would be a short-lived fad. The music surpassed these predictions and became a genre that defines an era.

July 9, 1955 is the starting point of the research of this book. That is the landmark date of rock and roll's first #1 hit on a pop chart: "Rock Around The Clock" by Bill Haley And His Comets hit #1 on *Billboard* magazine's "Best Sellers in Stores" popular record chart. That song on that date heralded a new era in which rockabilly, Country and R&B music became driving forces in mainstream Top 40 radio.

Who determined the 1,000 biggest hits of the rock era? Was it a select group of critics? Is it a list of my favorites? No, you voted each week for your favorites. Your purchases of these records and your requests to your favorite radio stations resulted in airplay – all of which was tallied on a weekly basis by *Billboard*, the #1 music trade magazine in the world. We've researched all of these charts through the years. #1 thru #975 were all #1 hits – in fact, herein is every #1 hit since "Rock Around The Clock" began this hit parade. The final 25 hits in the countdown settled in at #2.

If you're looking for a list of top songs from your year of graduation or marriage, or any milestone event, then check out our "Top 40 Hits" guide following the Top 1000 ranking. Here you'll find a listing that goes well beyond the #1 hits of a particular year. For some years, the 40 biggest hits include those that peaked at position 7.

Popular music of the rock era encompasses many genres. The countdown begins at #1000 with Chingy, a 23-year-old rapper from St. Louis who had the party rap anthem of the summer of 2003 with "Right Thurr." #999 is a powerful rock opera penned by Jim Steinman, "It's All Coming Back To Me Now," performed by Celine Dion. Country-pop fans will be pleased to hear Faith Hill at #998 with "Breathe." Then, the all-time frat-party song "Louie Louie" by The Kingsmen comes in at #997. And on it goes, an eclectic mix.

While browsing through the listing, you'll find some interesting trivial tidbits, such as:

> - Elvis Presley with the most Top 100 hits: 5
> - The Rolling Stones and The Beatles – back-to-back at #863 & 864
> - Janet Jackson and Michael Jackson – back-to-back at #955 & 956
> - 7 different artists with their own back-to-back hits
> - "Half-Breed" near the halfway mark at #502
> - "Sugartime" and "Sugar Sugar" at #183 & 184
> - "Again" and "Together Again" at #393 & 395
> - "Good Vibrations" and "Good Lovin'" at #844 & 845
> - "Ms. Jackson," "Diana" and "Tom Dooley" at #657-659
> - Or, how about "Don't" "Jump" at #131 & 132

So then, here they are – in rank order – America's Top 1000 songs as voted by you, the reader. Enjoy the tour!

JOEL WHITBURN

THE RANKING SYSTEM

All chart data is compiled from *Billboard's* pop singles charts. See the synopsis below for a breakdown of those charts.

Our ranking methodology is based on the most-quoted of all chart statistics — the peak position. Basically, the peak position of a song title and the weeks it held that position determine its final ranking.

Following is the ranking formula:

1) All songs that peaked at #1 are listed first, followed by songs that peaked at #2, and so on.
2) Ties among these #1 (and #2) songs are broken in the following order:
   a) Total weeks at the peak position
   b) Total weeks in the Top 10
   c) Total weeks in the Top 40
   d) Total weeks charted

If ties still existed, a computerized inverse point system calculated a point total for each song based on its weekly chart positions. For each week that a song appeared on the charts, it earned points according to each of its weekly chart positions (#1=100, #2=99 points, etc.). The sum of these points broke any remaining ties.

Below is a synopsis of *Billboard's* pop singles charts which were researched commencing with the first year of the rock era — 1955. For a song that appeared on more than one of the multiple 1950s weekly charts (Juke Box, Best Sellers, Jockeys or Top 100), its peak position is determined by the chart on which it achieved its highest peak.

DATE	CHART	POSITIONS
7/9/55– 6/17/57 (final chart)	**MOST PLAYED JUKE BOX RECORDS**	15-30
7/9/55– 10/13/58 (final chart)	**BEST SELLERS IN STORES**	20-50
7/9/55– 7/28/58 (final chart)	**MOST PLAYED BY JOCKEYS**	15-30
11/12/55– 7/28/58 (final chart)	**TOP 100**	100
8/4/58 (first chart)	**HOT 100** First, all-encompassing chart.	100
11/30/91	**HOT 100** *Billboard* begins using actual monitored airplay (from Broadcast Data Systems), actual sales figures (from SoundScan) and playlists from small-market radio stations to compile the chart.	100
12/5/98	**HOT 100** *Billboard* begins to include airplay hits that are not commercially available as singles.	100

THE PICTORIAL RANKING

These are the Top 1000 hits compiled from *Billboard's* pop singles charts from July 9, 1955 through December 24, 2005.

1.
One Sweet Day...
Mariah Carey & Boyz II Men
1995: #**1** - 16 wks.

2.
Macarena...
Los Del Rio
1996: #**1** - 14 wks.

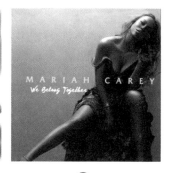

3.
We Belong Together...
Mariah Carey
2005: #**1** - 14 wks.

4.
I'll Make Love To You...
Boyz II Men
1994: #**1** - 14 wks.

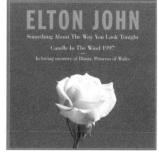

5.
Candle In The Wind 1997/Something
About The Way You Look Tonight...
Elton John
1997: #**1** - 14 wks.

6.
I Will Always Love You...
Whitney Houston
1992: #**1** - 14 wks.

7.
End of the Road...
Boyz II Men
1992: #**1** - 13 wks.

8.
The Boy Is Mine...
Brandy & Monica
1998: #**1** - 13 wks.

9.
Smooth...
Santana Feat. Rob Thomas
1999: #**1** - 12 wks.

TOP 1000 — 1955-2005

10.
Yeah!...
Usher Featuring Lil' Jon & Ludacris
2004: #**1** - 12 wks.

11.
Lose Yourself...
Eminem
2002: #**1** - 12 wks.

12.
Un-Break My Heart...
Toni Braxton
1996: #**1** - 11 wks.

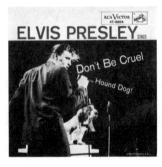

13.
Don't Be Cruel/Hound Dog...
Elvis Presley
1956: #**1** - 11 wks.

14.
I Swear...
All-4-One
1994: #**1** - 11 wks.

15.
I'll Be Missing You...
Puff Daddy & Faith Evans
1997: #**1** - 11 wks.

16.
Independent Women Part I...
Destiny's Child
2000: #**1** - 11 wks.

17.
Dilemma...
Nelly Featuring Kelly Rowland
2002: #**1** - 10 wks.

18.
Maria Maria...
Santana Feat. The Product G&B
2000: #**1** - 10 wks.

TOP 1000 — 1955-2005

19.
Foolish...
Ashanti
2002: #**1** - 10 wks.

20.
Singing The Blues...
Guy Mitchell
1956: #**1** - 10 wks.

21.
Physical...
Olivia Newton-John
1981: #**1** - 10 wks.

22.
Gold Digger...
Kanye West featuring Jamie Foxx
2005: #**1** - 10 wks.

23.
You Light Up My Life...
Debby Boone
1977: #**1** - 10 wks.

24.
Let Me Love You...
Mario
2005: #**1** - 9 wks.

25.
Hey Ya!...
OutKast
2003: #**1** - 9 wks.

26.
In Da Club...
50 Cent
2003: #**1** - 9 wks.

27.
Mack The Knife...
Bobby Darin
1959: #**1** - 9 wks.

TOP 1000 — 1955-2005

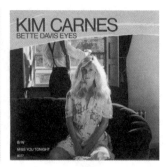

28.
Baby Boy...
Beyoncé Featuring Sean Paul
2003: #**1** - 9 wks.

29.
All Shook Up...
Elvis Presley
1957: #**1** - 9 wks.

30.
Bette Davis Eyes...
Kim Carnes
1981: #**1** - 9 wks.

31.
Candy Shop...
50 Cent Featuring Olivia
2005: #**1** - 9 wks.

32.
Hey Jude...
The Beatles
1968: #**1** - 9 wks.

33.
Endless Love...
Diana Ross & Lionel Richie
1981: #**1** - 9 wks.

34.
The Theme From "A Summer
Place"...*Percy Faith*
1960: #**1** - 9 wks.

35.
Rock Around The Clock...
Bill Haley And His Comets
1955: #**1** - 8 wks.

36.
Burn...
Usher
2004: #**1** - 8 wks.

TOP 1000 — 1955-2005

37.
Crazy In Love...
Beyoncé (Featuring Jay-Z)
2003: #**1** - 8 wks.

38.
Fantasy...
Mariah Carey
1995: #**1** - 8 wks.

39.
The Wayward Wind...
Gogi Grant
1956: #**1** - 8 wks.

40.
Sixteen Tons...
"Tennessee" Ernie Ford
1955: #**1** - 8 wks.

41.
Heartbreak Hotel...
Elvis Presley
1956: #**1** - 8 wks.

42.
Dreamlover...
Mariah Carey
1993: #**1** - 8 wks.

43.
That's The Way Love Goes...
Janet Jackson
1993: #**1** - 8 wks.

44.
Every Breath You Take...
The Police
1983: #**1** - 8 wks.

45.
Jump...
Kris Kross
1992: #**1** - 8 wks.

TOP 1000 — 1955-2005

46.
Night Fever...
Bee Gees
1978: #**1** - 8 wks.

47.
Tha Crossroads...
Bone thugs-n-harmony
1996: #**1** - 8 wks.

48.
Tonight's The Night (Gonna Be
Alright)...*Rod Stewart*
1976: #**1** - 8 wks.

49.
Waterfalls...
TLC
1995: #**1** - 7 wks.

50.
Hot In Herre...
Nelly
2002: #**1** - 7 wks.

51.
Goodies...
Ciara featuring Petey Pablo
2004: #**1** - 7 wks.

52.
Love Letters In The Sand...
Pat Boone
1957: #**1** - 7 wks.

53.
Take A Bow...
Madonna
1995: #**1** - 7 wks.

54.
Can't Help Falling In Love...
UB40
1993: #**1** - 7 wks.

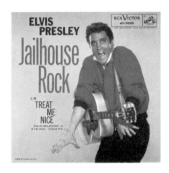

55.
Jailhouse Rock...
Elvis Presley
1957: #**1** - 7 wks.

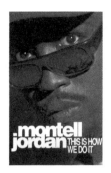

56.
This Is How We Do It...
Montell Jordan
1995: #**1** - 7 wks.

57.
All For You...
Janet Jackson
2001: #**1** - 7 wks.

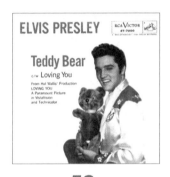

58.
(Let Me Be Your) Teddy Bear...
Elvis Presley
1957: #**1** - 7 wks.

59.
Informer...
Snow
1993: #**1** - 7 wks.

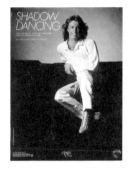

60.
Shadow Dancing...
Andy Gibb
1978: #**1** - 7 wks.

61.
At The Hop...
Danny & The Juniors
1958: #**1** - 7 wks.

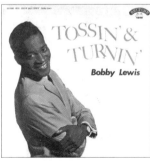

62.
Tossin' And Turnin'...
Bobby Lewis
1961: #**1** - 7 wks.

63.
I Love Rock 'N Roll...
Joan Jett & The Blackhearts
1982: #**1** - 7 wks.

64.
Ebony And Ivory...
Paul McCartney (w/ Stevie Wonder)
1982: #**1** - 7 wks.

65.
I Want To Hold Your Hand...
The Beatles
1964: #**1** - 7 wks.

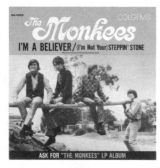

66.
I'm A Believer...
The Monkees
1966: #**1** - 7 wks.

67.
Billie Jean...
Michael Jackson
1983: #**1** - 7 wks.

68.
I Heard It Through The Grapevine...
Marvin Gaye
1968: #**1** - 7 wks.

69.
(Everything I Do) I Do It For You...
Bryan Adams
1991: #**1** - 7 wks.

70.
Black Or White...
Michael Jackson
1991: #**1** - 7 wks.

71.
The Sign...
Ace Of Base
1994: #**1** - 6 wks.

72.
U Got It Bad...
Usher
2001: #**1** - 6 wks.

73.
Family Affair...
Mary J. Blige
2001: #**1** - 6 wks.

74.
Because You Loved Me...
Celine Dion
1996: #**1** - 6 wks.

75.
Fallin'...
Alicia Keys
2001: #**1** - 6 wks.

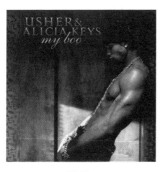

76.
My Boo...
Usher & Alicia Keys
2004: #**1** - 6 wks.

77.
On Bended Knee...
Boyz II Men
1994: #**1** - 6 wks.

78.
Love Is A Many-Splendored Thing...
Four Aces
1955: #**1** - 6 wks.

79.
Can't Nobody Hold Me Down...
Puff Daddy Featuring Mase
1997: #**1** - 6 wks.

80.
Rock And Roll Waltz...
Kay Starr
1956: #**1** - 6 wks.

81.
The Poor People Of Paris...
Les Baxter
1956: #**1** - 6 wks.

82.
The Yellow Rose Of Texas...
Mitch Miller
1955: #**1** - 6 wks.

83.
Ain't It Funny...
Jennifer Lopez featuring Ja Rule
2002: #**1** - 6 wks.

84.
Le Freak...
Chic
1978: #**1** - 6 wks.

85.
Memories Are Made Of This...
Dean Martin
1956: #**1** - 6 wks.

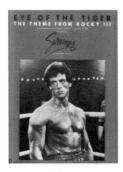

86.
Eye Of The Tiger...
Survivor
1982: #**1** - 6 wks.

87.
Flashdance...What A Feeling...
Irene Cara
1983: #**1** - 6 wks.

88.
April Love...
Pat Boone
1957: #**1** - 6 wks.

89.
Lady...
Kenny Rogers
1980: #**1** - 6 wks.

90.
Say Say Say...
Paul McCartney & Michael Jackson
1983: #**1** - 6 wks.

91.
The Battle Of New Orleans...
Johnny Horton
1959: #**1** - 6 wks.

92.
Young Love...
Tab Hunter
1957: #**1** - 6 wks.

93.
Centerfold...
The J. Geils Band
1982: #**1** - 6 wks.

94.
Call Me...
Blondie
1980: #**1** - 6 wks.

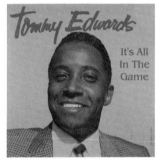

95.
It's All In The Game...
Tommy Edwards
1958: #**1** - 6 wks.

96.
My Sharona...
The Knack
1979: #**1** - 6 wks.

97.
Aquarius/Let The Sunshine In...
The 5th Dimension
1969: #**1** - 6 wks.

98.
The First Time Ever I Saw Your
Face...*Roberta Flack*
1972: #**1** - 6 wks.

99.
Alone Again (Naturally)...
Gilbert O'Sullivan
1972: #**1** - 6 wks.

TOP 1000 — 1955-2005

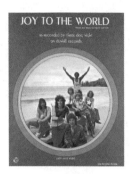

100.
Joy To The World...
Three Dog Night
1971: #**1** - 6 wks.

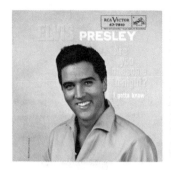

101.
Are You Lonesome To-night?...
Elvis Presley
1960: #**1** - 6 wks.

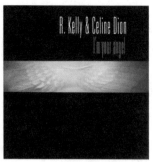

102.
I'm Your Angel...
R. Kelly & Celine Dion
1998: #**1** - 6 wks.

103.
The Purple People Eater...
Sheb Wooley
1958: #**1** - 6 wks.

104.
Bridge Over Troubled Water...
Simon & Garfunkel
1970: #**1** - 6 wks.

105.
Like A Virgin...
Madonna
1984: #**1** - 6 wks.

106.
In The Year 2525...
Zager & Evans
1969: #**1** - 6 wks.

107.
Too Close...
Next
1998: #**1** - 5 wks.

108.
I'm Real...
Jennifer Lopez featuring Ja Rule
2001: #**1** - 5 wks.

109.
Tammy...
Debbie Reynolds
1957: #**1** - 5 wks.

110.
The First Night...
Monica
1998: #**1** - 5 wks.

111.
Baby Got Back...
Sir Mix-A-Lot
1992: #**1** - 5 wks.

112.
If You Had My Love...
Jennifer Lopez
1999: #**1** - 5 wks.

113.
Love Me Tender...
Elvis Presley
1956: #**1** - 5 wks.

114.
Genie In A Bottle...
Christina Aguilera
1999: #**1** - 5 wks.

115.
My Prayer...
The Platters
1956: #**1** - 5 wks.

116.
(Just Like) Starting Over...
John Lennon
1980: #**1** - 5 wks.

117.
I'd Do Anything For Love (But I Won't
Do That)...*Meat Loaf*
1993: #**1** - 5 wks.

118.
Livin' La Vida Loca...
Ricky Martin
1999: #**1** - 5 wks.

119.
Save The Best For Last...
Vanessa Williams
1992: #**1** - 5 wks.

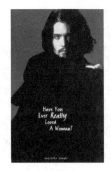

120.
Have You Ever Really Loved A
Woman?...*Bryan Adams*
1995: #**1** - 5 wks.

121.
Best Of My Love...
Emotions
1977: #**1** - 5 wks.

122.
Lady Marmalade...
*Christina Aguilera, Lil' Kim,
Mya and P!nk*
2001: #**1** - 5 wks.

123.
All I Have To Do Is Dream...
The Everly Brothers
1958: #**1** - 5 wks.

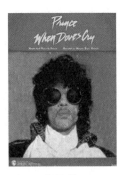

124.
When Doves Cry...
Prince
1984: #**1** - 5 wks.

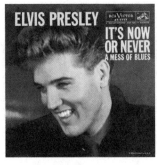

125.
It's Now Or Never...
Elvis Presley
1960: #**1** - 5 wks.

126.
Tequila...
The Champs
1958: #**1** - 5 wks.

127.
I'll Be There...
The Jackson 5
1970: #**1** - 5 wks.

128.
Silly Love Songs...
Wings
1976: #**1** - 5 wks.

129.
Maggie May...
Rod Stewart
1971: #**1** - 5 wks.

130.
I Can't Stop Loving You...
Ray Charles
1962: #**1** - 5 wks.

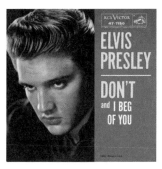

131.
Don't...
Elvis Presley
1958: #**1** - 5 wks.

132.
Jump...
Van Halen
1984: #**1** - 5 wks.

133.
Bad Girls...
Donna Summer
1979: #**1** - 5 wks.

134.
Love Is Blue...
Paul Mauriat
1968: #**1** - 5 wks.

135.
It's Too Late...
Carole King
1971: #**1** - 5 wks.

136.
Venus...
Frankie Avalon
1959: #**1** - 5 wks.

137.
Big Girls Don't Cry...
The 4 Seasons
1962: #**1** - 5 wks.

138.
Run It!...
Chris Brown
2005: #**1** - 5 wks.

139.
Nel Blu Dipinto Di Blu (Volaré)...
Domenico Modugno
1958: #**1** - 5 wks.

140.
Big Bad John...
Jimmy Dean
1961: #**1** - 5 wks.

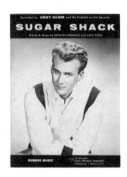

141.
Sugar Shack...
Jimmy Gilmer & The Fireballs
1963: #**1** - 5 wks.

142.
Honey...
Bobby Goldsboro
1968: #**1** - 5 wks.

143.
Rush, Rush...
Paula Abdul
1991: #**1** - 5 wks.

144.
To Sir With Love...
Lulu
1967: #**1** - 5 wks.

145.
Cathy's Clown...
The Everly Brothers
1960: #**1** - 5 wks.

146.
Killing Me Softly With His Song...
Roberta Flack
1973: #**1** - 5 wks.

147.
People Got To Be Free...
The Rascals
1968: #**1** - 5 wks.

148.
One Bad Apple...
The Osmonds
1971: #**1** - 5 wks.

149.
Get Back...
The Beatles with Billy Preston
1969: #**1** - 5 wks.

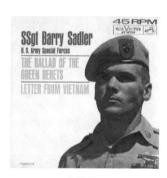

150.
The Ballad Of The Green Berets...
SSgt Barry Sadler
1966: #**1** - 5 wks.

151.
Sherry...
The 4 Seasons
1962: #**1** - 5 wks.

152.
Can't Buy Me Love...
The Beatles
1964: #**1** - 5 wks.

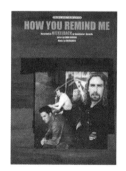

153.
How You Remind Me...
Nickelback
2001: #**1** - 4 wks.

154.
Creep...
TLC
1995: #**1** - 4 wks.

155.
Hollaback Girl...
Gwen Stefani
2005: #**1** - 4 wks.

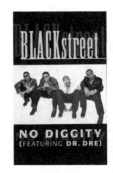

156.
No Diggity...
BLACKstreet (Featuring Dr. Dre)
1996: #**1** - 4 wks.

157.
Autumn Leaves...
Roger Williams
1955: #**1** - 4 wks.

158.
I Knew I Loved You...
Savage Garden
2000: #**1** - 4 wks.

159.
No Scrubs...
TLC
1999: #**1** - 4 wks.

160.
Lisbon Antigua...
Nelson Riddle
1956: #**1** - 4 wks.

161.
The Power Of Love...
Celine Dion
1994: #**1** - 4 wks.

162.
Believe...
Cher
1999: #**1** - 4 wks.

  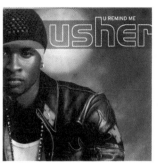

163.
Hero...
Mariah Carey
1993: #**1** - 4 wks.

164.
I Just Want To Be Your Everything...
Andy Gibb
1977: #**1** - 4 wks.

165.
U Remind Me...
Usher
2001: #**1** - 4 wks.

  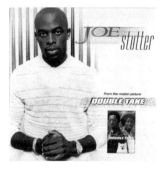

166.
Angel Of Mine...
Monica
1999: #**1** - 4 wks.

167.
Wannabe...
Spice Girls
1997: #**1** - 4 wks.

168.
Stutter...
Joe (Featuring Mystikal)
2001: #**1** - 4 wks.

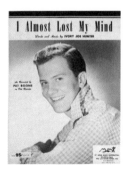  

169.
I Almost Lost My Mind...
Pat Boone
1956: #**1** - 4 wks.

170.
Upside Down...
Diana Ross
1980: #**1** - 4 wks.

171.
Honeycomb...
Jimmie Rodgers
1957: #**1** - 4 wks.

172.
Stayin' Alive...
Bee Gees
1978: #**1** - 4 wks.

173.
21 Questions...
50 Cent Feat. Nate Dogg
2003: #**1** - 4 wks.

174.
Raindrops Keep Fallin' On My
Head...*B.J. Thomas*
1970: #**1** - 4 wks.

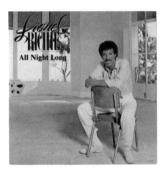

175.
All Night Long (All Night)...
Lionel Richie
1983: #**1** - 4 wks.

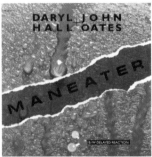

176.
Maneater...
Daryl Hall & John Oates
1982: #**1** - 4 wks.

177.
Shake Ya Tailfeather...
Nelly/P. Diddy/Murphy Lee
2003: #**1** - 4 wks.

178.
Bump N' Grind...
R. Kelly
1994: #**1** - 4 wks.

179.
Music...
Madonna
2000: #**1** - 4 wks.

180.
Wake Up Little Susie...
The Everly Brothers
1957: #**1** - 4 wks.

181.
All I Have...
Jennifer Lopez Featuring LL Cool J
2003: **#1** - 4 wks.

182.
Another Brick In The Wall Part II...
Pink Floyd
1980: **#1** - 4 wks.

183.
Sugartime...
The McGuire Sisters
1958: **#1** - 4 wks.

184.
Sugar, Sugar...
The Archies
1969: **#1** - 4 wks.

185.
Da Ya Think I'm Sexy?...
Rod Stewart
1979: **#1** - 4 wks.

186.
Kiss You All Over...
Exile
1978: **#1** - 4 wks.

187.
Crazy Little Thing Called Love...
Queen
1980: **#1** - 4 wks.

188.
Total Eclipse Of The Heart...
Bonnie Tyler
1983: **#1** - 4 wks.

189.
Tie A Yellow Ribbon Round The Ole
Oak Tree...*Dawn feat. Tony Orlando*
1973: **#1** - 4 wks.

190.
American Pie - Parts I & II...
Don McLean
1972: **#1** - 4 wks.

191.
(They Long To Be) Close To You...
Carpenters
1970: **#1** - 4 wks.

192.
(Sittin' On) The Dock Of The Bay...
Otis Redding
1968: **#1** - 4 wks.

193.
Honky Tonk Women...
The Rolling Stones
1969: **#1** - 4 wks.

194.
Down Under...
Men At Work
1983: **#1** - 4 wks.

195.
That's What Friends Are For...
Dionne & Friends
1986: **#1** - 4 wks.

196.
Jack & Diane...
John Cougar
1982: **#1** - 4 wks.

197.
Because I Love You (The Postman Song)...*Stevie B*
1990: **#1** - 4 wks.

198.
Reunited...
Peaches & Herb
1979: **#1** - 4 wks.

199.
Nothing Compares 2 U...
Sinéad O'Connor
1990: #**1** - 4 wks.

200.
Stagger Lee...
Lloyd Price
1959: #**1** - 4 wks.

201.
I Don't Want To Miss A Thing...
Aerosmith
1998: #**1** - 4 wks.

202.
Another Day In Paradise...
Phil Collins
1989: #**1** - 4 wks.

203.
The Three Bells...
The Browns
1959: #**1** - 4 wks.

204.
Lonely Boy...
Paul Anka
1959: #**1** - 4 wks.

205.
How Can You Mend A Broken
Heart...*The Bee Gees*
1971: #**1** - 4 wks.

206.
Stuck On You...
Elvis Presley
1960: #**1** - 4 wks.

207.
Roses Are Red (My Love)...
Bobby Vinton
1962: #**1** - 4 wks.

208.
My Sweet Lord...
George Harrison
1970: #**1** - 4 wks.

209.
Daydream Believer...
The Monkees
1967: #**1** - 4 wks.

210.
Rock With You...
Michael Jackson
1980: #**1** - 4 wks.

211.
Magic...
Olivia Newton-John
1980: #**1** - 4 wks.

212.
Say You, Say Me...
Lionel Richie
1985: #**1** - 4 wks.

213.
Funkytown...
Lipps, Inc.
1980: #**1** - 4 wks.

214.
Faith...
George Michael
1987: #**1** - 4 wks.

215.
My Love...
Paul McCartney & Wings
1973: #**1** - 4 wks.

216.
Everyday People...
Sly & The Family Stone
1969: #**1** - 4 wks.

217.
Without You...
Nilsson
1972: #**1** - 4 wks.

218.
He's Got The Whole World (In His Hands)...*Laurie London*
1958: #**1** - 4 wks.

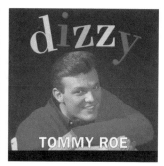

219.
Dizzy...
Tommy Roe
1969: #**1** - 4 wks.

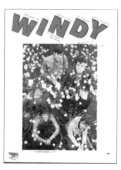

220.
Windy...
The Association
1967: #**1** - 4 wks.

221.
Runaway...
Del Shannon
1961: #**1** - 4 wks.

222.
He's So Fine...
The Chiffons
1963: #**1** - 4 wks.

223.
(I Can't Get No) Satisfaction...
The Rolling Stones
1965: #**1** - 4 wks.

224.
Ode To Billie Joe...
Bobbie Gentry
1967: #**1** - 4 wks.

225.
Dominique...
The Singing Nun
1963: #**1** - 4 wks.

226.
There! I've Said It Again...
Bobby Vinton
1964: #**1** - 4 wks.

227.
Somethin' Stupid...
Nancy Sinatra & Frank Sinatra
1967: #**1** - 4 wks.

228.
Groovin'...
The Young Rascals
1967: #**1** - 4 wks.

229.
Come On Over Baby (all I want is
you)...*Christina Aguilera*
2000: #**1** - 4 wks.

230.
Walk Like An Egyptian...
Bangles
1986: #**1** - 4 wks.

231.
Don't Go Breaking My Heart...
Elton John & Kiki Dee
1976: #**1** - 4 wks.

232.
I Can See Clearly Now...
Johnny Nash
1972: #**1** - 4 wks.

233.
Miss You Much...
Janet Jackson
1989: #**1** - 4 wks.

234.
Disco Lady...
Johnnie Taylor
1976: #**1** - 4 wks.

235.
The Letter...
The Box Tops
1967: #**1** - 4 wks.

236.
We Are The World...
USA for Africa
1985: #**1** - 4 wks.

237.
Come Softly To Me...
The Fleetwoods
1959: #**1** - 4 wks.

238.
This Guy's In Love With You...
Herb Alpert
1968: #**1** - 4 wks.

239.
Baby Love...
The Supremes
1964: #**1** - 4 wks.

240.
Vision Of Love...
Mariah Carey
1990: #**1** - 4 wks.

241.
Roll With It...
Steve Winwood
1988: #**1** - 4 wks.

242.
Livin' On A Prayer...
Bon Jovi
1987: #**1** - 4 wks.

243.
Love Will Keep Us Together...
The Captain & Tennille
1975: #**1** - 4 wks.

244.
The Chipmunk Song...
The Chipmunks
1958: #**1** - 4 wks.

245.
Yesterday...
The Beatles
1965: #**1** - 4 wks.

246.
The Twist...
Chubby Checker
1960: #**1** - 3 wks.

247.
Gangsta's Paradise...
Coolio featuring L.V.
1995: #**1** - 3 wks.

248.
The Green Door...
Jim Lowe
1956: #**1** - 3 wks.

249.
Drop It Like It's Hot...
Snoop Dogg featuring Pharrell
2004: #**1** - 3 wks.

250.
Get Busy...
Sean Paul
2003: #**1** - 3 wks.

251.
Lean Back...
Terror Squad
2004: #**1** - 3 wks.

252.
How Deep Is Your Love...
Bee Gees
1977: #**1** - 3 wks.

253.
Stay (I Missed You)...
Lisa Loeb & Nine Stories
1994: #**1** - 3 wks.

254.
Moonglow and Theme From
"Picnic"...
Morris Stoloff
1956: #**1** - 3 wks.

255.
Another One Bites The Dust...
Queen
1980: #**1** - 3 wks.

256.
Unpretty...
TLC
1999: #**1** - 3 wks.

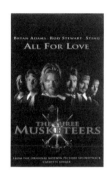

257.
All For Love...
Bryan Adams/Rod Stewart/Sting
1994: #**1** - 3 wks.

258.
Hot Stuff...
Donna Summer
1979: #**1** - 3 wks.

259.
Love Theme From "A Star
Is Born" (Evergreen)...
Barbra Streisand
1977: #**1** - 3 wks.

260.
I Will Survive...
Gloria Gaynor
1979: #**1** - 3 wks.

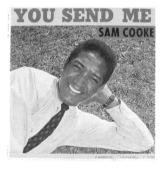

261.
You Send Me...
Sam Cooke
1957: #**1** - 3 wks.

262.
All My Life...
K-Ci & JoJo
1998: **#1** - 3 wks.

263.
Don't You Want Me...
The Human League
1982: **#1** - 3 wks.

264.
Doesn't Really Matter...
Janet
2000: **#1** - 3 wks.

265.
MMMBop...
Hanson
1997: **#1** - 3 wks.

266.
Witch Doctor...
David Seville
1958: **#1** - 3 wks.

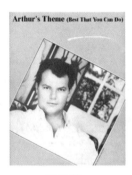

267.
Arthur's Theme (Best
That You Can Do)...
Christopher Cross
1981: **#1** - 3 wks.

268.
Boogie Oogie Oogie...
A Taste Of Honey
1978: **#1** - 3 wks.

269.
I'm Too Sexy...
*R*S*F (Right Said Fred)*
1992: **#1** - 3 wks.

270.
Say My Name...
Destiny's Child
2000: **#1** - 3 wks.

271.
Woman In Love...
Barbra Streisand
1980: #**1** - 3 wks.

272.
I'm Sorry...
Brenda Lee
1960: #**1** - 3 wks.

273.
To Know Him, Is To Love Him...
The Teddy Bears
1958: #**1** - 3 wks.

274.
Footloose...
Kenny Loggins
1984: #**1** - 3 wks.

275.
Coming Up (Live At Glasgow)...
Paul McCartney & Wings
1980: #**1** - 3 wks.

276.
I Think I Love You...
The Partridge Family
1970: #**1** - 3 wks.

277.
Knock Three Times...
Dawn
1971: #**1** - 3 wks.

278.
Peppermint Twist - Part I...
Joey Dee & the Starliters
1962: #**1** - 3 wks.

279.
You're So Vain...
Carly Simon
1973: #**1** - 3 wks.

280.
What's Love Got To Do With It...
Tina Turner
1984: #**1** - 3 wks.

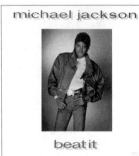

281.
Beat It...
Michael Jackson
1983: #**1** - 3 wks.

282.
Play That Funky Music...
Wild Cherry
1976: #**1** - 3 wks.

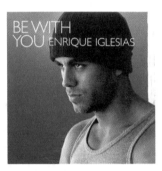

283.
Be With You...
Enrique Iglesias
2000: #**1** - 3 wks.

284.
Baby Come Back...
Player
1978: #**1** - 3 wks.

285.
Against All Odds (Take A
Look At Me Now)...
Phil Collins
1984: #**1** - 3 wks.

286.
Escape (The Pina Colada Song)...
Rupert Holmes
1979: #**1** - 3 wks.

287.
Smoke Gets In Your Eyes...
The Platters
1959: #**1** - 3 wks.

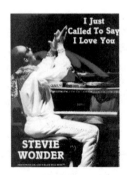

288.
I Just Called To Say I Love You...
Stevie Wonder
1984: #**1** - 3 wks.

289.
Wonderland By Night...
Bert Kaempfert
1961: #**1** - 3 wks.

290.
Running Bear...
Johnny Preston
1960: #**1** - 3 wks.

291.
Ghostbusters...
Ray Parker Jr.
1984: #**1** - 3 wks.

292.
Butterfly...
Andy Williams
1957: #**1** - 3 wks.

293.
Brand New Key...
Melanie
1971: #**1** - 3 wks.

294.
Winchester Cathedral...
The New Vaudeville Band
1966: #**1** - 3 wks.

295.
A Horse With No Name...
America
1972: #**1** - 3 wks.

296.
To Be With You...
Mr. Big
1992: #**1** - 3 wks.

297.
The Way We Were...
Barbra Streisand
1974: #**1** - 3 wks.

298.
Careless Whisper...
Wham! feat. George Michael
1985: #**1** - 3 wks.

299.
Karma Chameleon...
Culture Club
1984: #**1** - 3 wks.

300.
MacArthur Park...
Donna Summer
1978: #**1** - 3 wks.

301.
Save The Last Dance For Me...
The Drifters
1960: #**1** - 3 wks.

302.
Crocodile Rock...
Elton John
1973: #**1** - 3 wks.

303.
Light My Fire...
The Doors
1967: #**1** - 3 wks.

304.
Too Much...
Elvis Presley
1957: #**1** - 3 wks.

305.
Baby Don't Get Hooked On Me...
Mac Davis
1972: #**1** - 3 wks.

306.
Go Away Little Girl...
Donny Osmond
1971: #**1** - 3 wks.

307.
Family Affair...
Sly & The Family Stone
1971: #**1** - 3 wks.

308.
Ain't No Mountain High Enough...
Diana Ross
1970: #**1** - 3 wks.

309.
Happy Together...
The Turtles
1967: #**1** - 3 wks.

310.
Hey Paula...
Paul & Paula
1963: #**1** - 3 wks.

311.
My Boyfriend's Back...
The Angels
1963: #**1** - 3 wks.

312.
Honey...
Mariah Carey
1997: #**1** - 3 wks.

313.
Kiss On My List...
Daryl Hall & John Oates
1981: #**1** - 3 wks.

314.
Vogue...
Madonna
1990: #**1** - 3 wks.

315.
Seasons In The Sun...
Terry Jacks
1974: #**1** - 3 wks.

316.
Alone...
Heart
1987: #**1** - 3 wks.

317.
Wake Me Up Before You Go-Go...
Wham!
1984: #**1** - 3 wks.

318.
Every Rose Has Its Thorn...
Poison
1988: #**1** - 3 wks.

319.
Hypnotize...
The Notorious B.I.G.
1997: #**1** - 3 wks.

320.
Can't Fight This Feeling...
REO Speedwagon
1985: #**1** - 3 wks.

321.
Escapade...
Janet Jackson
1990: #**1** - 3 wks.

322.
Pony Time...
Chubby Checker
1961: #**1** - 3 wks.

323.
Me And Mrs. Jones...
Billy Paul
1972: #**1** - 3 wks.

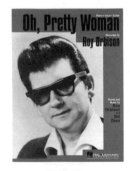

324.
Oh, Pretty Woman...
Roy Orbison
1964: #**1** - 3 wks.

325.
American Woman...
The Guess Who
1970: #**1** - 3 wks.

326.
Wedding Bell Blues...
The 5th Dimension
1969: #**1** - 3 wks.

327.
Money For Nothing...
Dire Straits
1985: #**1** - 3 wks.

328.
With Or Without You...
U2
1987: #**1** - 3 wks.

329.
Sir Duke...
Stevie Wonder
1977: #**1** - 3 wks.

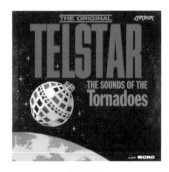

330.
Telstar...
The Tornadoes
1962: #**1** - 3 wks.

331.
War...
Edwin Starr
1970: #**1** - 3 wks.

332.
The Lion Sleeps Tonight...
The Tokens
1961: #**1** - 3 wks.

333.
Soldier Boy...
The Shirelles
1962: #**1** - 3 wks.

334.
The Streak...
Ray Stevens
1974: #**1** - 3 wks.

335.
Blue Velvet...
Bobby Vinton
1963: #**1** - 3 wks.

336.
Hey! Baby...
Bruce Channel
1962: #**1** - 3 wks.

337.
Sukiyaki...
Kyu Sakamoto
1963: #**1** - 3 wks.

338.
Duke Of Earl...
Gene Chandler
1962: #**1** - 3 wks.

339.
Turn! Turn! Turn! (To Everything There
Is A Season)...*The Byrds*
1965: #**1** - 3 wks.

340.
Blue Moon...
The Marcels
1961: #**1** - 3 wks.

341.
I Will Follow Him...
Little Peggy March
1963: #**1** - 3 wks.

342.
(You're My) Soul And Inspiration...
The Righteous Brothers
1966: #**1** - 3 wks.

343.
Monday, Monday...
The Mamas And The Papas
1966: #**1** - 3 wks.

344.
Hello Goodbye...
The Beatles
1967: #**1** - 3 wks.

345.
The House Of The Rising Sun...
The Animals
1964: #**1** - 3 wks.

346.
Emotions...
Mariah Carey
1991: #**1** - 3 wks.

347.
Love Takes Time...
Mariah Carey
1990: #**1** - 3 wks.

348.
Straight Up...
Paula Abdul
1989: #**1** - 3 wks.

349.
The Candy Man...
Sammy Davis Jr.
1972: #**1** - 3 wks.

350.
Up Where We Belong...
Joe Cocker & Jennifer Warnes
1982: #**1** - 3 wks.

351.
On My Own...
Patti LaBelle and Michael McDonald
1986: #**1** - 3 wks.

TOP 1000 — 1955-2005

352.
Opposites Attract...
Paula Abdul
1990: **#1** - 3 wks.

353.
La Bamba...
Los Lobos
1987: **#1** - 3 wks.

354.
Lean On Me...
Bill Withers
1972: **#1** - 3 wks.

355.
Greatest Love Of All...
Whitney Houston
1986: **#1** - 3 wks.

356.
One More Try...
George Michael
1988: **#1** - 3 wks.

357.
Right Here Waiting...
Richard Marx
1989: **#1** - 3 wks.

358.
Shout...
Tears For Fears
1985: **#1** - 3 wks.

359.
Stuck With You...
Huey Lewis and the News
1986: **#1** - 3 wks.

360.
Fly, Robin, Fly...
Silver Convention
1975: **#1** - 3 wks.

361.
Rock Me Amadeus...
Falco
1986: #**1** - 3 wks.

362.
Lost In Your Eyes...
Debbie Gibson
1989: #**1** - 3 wks.

363.
Like A Prayer...
Madonna
1989: #**1** - 3 wks.

364.
Island Girl...
Elton John
1975: #**1** - 3 wks.

365.
Fingertips - Pt 2...
Little Stevie Wonder
1963: #**1** - 3 wks.

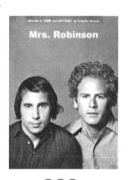

366.
Mrs. Robinson...
Simon And Garfunkel
1968: #**1** - 3 wks.

367.
Walk Like A Man...
The 4 Seasons
1963: #**1** - 3 wks.

368.
Take Good Care Of My Baby...
Bobby Vee
1961: #**1** - 3 wks.

369.
Step By Step...
New Kids On The Block
1990: #**1** - 3 wks.

370.
Chapel Of Love...
The Dixie Cups
1964: #**1** - 3 wks.

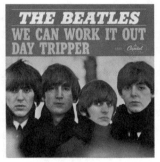

371.
We Can Work It Out...
The Beatles
1966: #**1** - 3 wks.

372.
Mrs. Brown You've Got
A Lovely Daughter...
Herman's Hermits
1965: #**1** - 3 wks.

373.
I Feel Fine...
The Beatles
1964: #**1** - 3 wks.

374.
I Got You Babe...
Sonny & Cher
1965: #**1** - 3 wks.

375.
Summer In The City...
The Lovin' Spoonful
1966: #**1** - 3 wks.

376.
Gettin' Jiggy Wit It...
Will Smith
1998: #**1** - 3 wks.

377.
How Am I Supposed To
Live Without You...
Michael Bolton
1990: #**1** - 3 wks.

378.
December, 1963 (Oh, What a Night)...
Four Seasons
1976: #**1** - 3 wks.

379.
50 Ways To Leave Your Lover...
Paul Simon
1976: #**1** - 3 wks.

380.
Cherish...
The Association
1966: #**1** - 3 wks.

381.
Help!...
The Beatles
1965: #**1** - 3 wks.

382.
(You're) Having My Baby...
Paul Anka
1974: #**1** - 3 wks.

383.
He Don't Love You
(Like I Love You)...
Tony Orlando & Dawn
1975: #**1** - 3 wks.

384.
Bad Blood...
Neil Sedaka
1975: #**1** - 3 wks.

385.
Truly Madly Deeply...
Savage Garden
1998: #**1** - 2 wks.

386.
Learnin' The Blues...
Frank Sinatra
1955: #**1** - 2 wks.

387.
Always On Time...
Ja Rule
2002: #**1** - 2 wks.

388.
It Wasn't Me...
Shaggy
2001: #**1** - 2 wks.

389.
Freak Me...
Silk
1993: #**1** - 2 wks.

390.
Always Be My Baby...
Mariah Carey
1996: #**1** - 2 wks.

391.
Here Comes The Hotstepper...
Ini Kamoze
1994: #**1** - 2 wks.

392.
Weak...
SWV (Sisters With Voices)
1993: #**1** - 2 wks.

393.
Again...
Janet Jackson
1993: #**1** - 2 wks.

394.
Ain't That A Shame...
Pat Boone
1955: #**1** - 2 wks.

395.
Together Again...
Janet
1998: #**1** - 2 wks.

396.
...Baby One More Time...
Britney Spears
1999: #**1** - 2 wks.

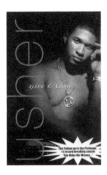

397.
Nice & Slow...
Usher
1998: **#1** - 2 wks.

398.
Round And Round...
Perry Como
1957: **#1** - 2 wks.

399.
Abracadabra...
The Steve Miller Band
1982: **#1** - 2 wks.

400.
The Great Pretender...
The Platters
1956: **#1** - 2 wks.

401.
Confessions Part II...
Usher
2004: **#1** - 2 wks.

402.
Have You Ever?...
Brandy
1999: **#1** - 2 wks.

403.
Incomplete...
Sisqó
2000: **#1** - 2 wks.

404.
Let's Get It On...
Marvin Gaye
1973: **#1** - 2 wks.

405.
Amazed...
Lonestar
2000: **#1** - 2 wks.

406.
Mo Money Mo Problems...
The Notorious B.I.G. Featuring Puff Daddy & Mase
1997: #**1** - 2 wks.

407.
Slow Motion...
Juvenile Featuring Soulja Slim
2004: #**1** - 2 wks.

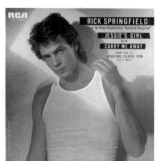

408.
Jessie's Girl...
Rick Springfield
1981: #**1** - 2 wks.

409.
Islands In The Stream...
Kenny Rogers with Dolly Parton
1983: #**1** - 2 wks.

410.
Hard To Say I'm Sorry...
Chicago
1982: #**1** - 2 wks.

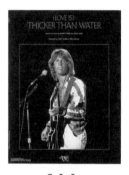

411.
(Love Is) Thicker Than Water...
Andy Gibb
1978: #**1** - 2 wks.

412.
It's Gonna Be Me...
*NSYNC
2000: #**1** - 2 wks.

413.
It's Still Rock And Roll To Me...
Billy Joel
1980: #**1** - 2 wks.

414.
Doo Wop (That Thing)...
Lauryn Hill
1998: #**1** - 2 wks.

TOP 1000 — 1955-2005

415.
Three Times A Lady...
Commodores
1978: #**1** - 2 wks.

416.
Ring My Bell...
Anita Ward
1979: #**1** - 2 wks.

417.
I Can't Get Next To You...
The Temptations
1969: #**1** - 2 wks.

418.
Love Child...
Diana Ross & The Supremes
1968: #**1** - 2 wks.

419.
Crimson And Clover...
Tommy James & The Shondells
1969: #**1** - 2 wks.

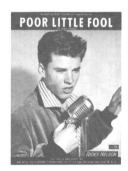

420.
Poor Little Fool...
Ricky Nelson
1958: #**1** - 2 wks.

421.
Babe...
Styx
1979: #**1** - 2 wks.

422.
She Loves You...
The Beatles
1964: #**1** - 2 wks.

423.
Let It Be...
The Beatles
1970: #**1** - 2 wks.

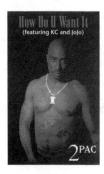

424.
How Do U Want It...
2 Pac (featuring KC and JoJo)
1996: #**1** - 2 wks.

425.
Hello...
Lionel Richie
1984: #**1** - 2 wks.

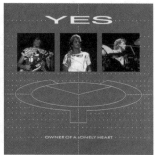

426.
Owner Of A Lonely Heart...
Yes
1984: #**1** - 2 wks.

427.
It's Only Make Believe...
Conway Twitty
1958: #**1** - 2 wks.

428.
Torn Between Two Lovers...
Mary MacGregor
1977: #**1** - 2 wks.

429.
Heartaches By The Number...
Guy Mitchell
1959: #**1** - 2 wks.

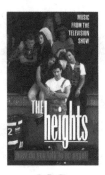

430.
How Do You Talk To An Angel...
The Heights
1992: #**1** - 2 wks.

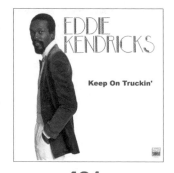

431.
Keep On Truckin' (Part 1)...
Eddie Kendricks
1973: #**1** - 2 wks.

432.
You Don't Bring Me Flowers...
Barbra & Neil
1978: #**1** - 2 wks.

TOP 1000 — 1955-2005

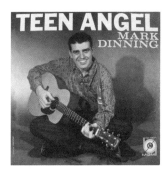

433.
Teen Angel...
Mark Dinning
1960: #**1** - 2 wks.

434.
My Heart Has A Mind Of Its Own...
Connie Francis
1960: #**1** - 2 wks.

435.
The Tears Of A Clown...
Smokey Robinson & The Miracles
1970: #**1** - 2 wks.

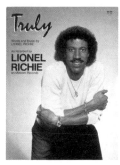

436.
Truly...
Lionel Richie
1982: #**1** - 2 wks.

437.
I Can't Help Myself...
Four Tops
1965: #**1** - 2 wks.

438.
Baby, Come To Me...
Patti Austin (with James Ingram)
1983: #**1** - 2 wks.

439.
I Love A Rainy Night...
Eddie Rabbitt
1981: #**1** - 2 wks.

440.
9 To 5...
Dolly Parton
1981: #**1** - 2 wks.

441.
Rhinestone Cowboy...
Glen Campbell
1975: #**1** - 2 wks.

442.
Kiss And Say Goodbye...
Manhattans
1976: #**1** - 2 wks.

443.
Gonna Make You Sweat
(Everybody Dance Now)...
C & C Music Factory
1991: #**1** - 2 wks.

444.
It Must Have Been Love...
Roxette
1990: #**1** - 2 wks.

445.
Private Eyes...
Daryl Hall & John Oates
1981: #**1** - 2 wks.

446.
Philadelphia Freedom...
The Elton John Band
1975: #**1** - 2 wks.

447.
If You Leave Me Now...
Chicago
1976: #**1** - 2 wks.

448.
Too Much Heaven...
Bee Gees
1979: #**1** - 2 wks.

449.
Out Of Touch...
Daryl Hall John Oates
1984: #**1** - 2 wks.

450.
Maniac...
Michael Sembello
1983: #**1** - 2 wks.

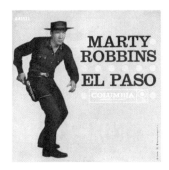

451.
El Paso...
Marty Robbins
1960: #**1** - 2 wks.

452.
Rise...
Herb Alpert
1979: #**1** - 2 wks.

453.
Broken Wings...
Mr. Mister
1985: #**1** - 2 wks.

454.
Time After Time...
Cyndi Lauper
1984: #**1** - 2 wks.

455.
Let's Hear It For The Boy...
Deniece Williams
1984: #**1** - 2 wks.

456.
Let's Go Crazy...
Prince and the Revolution
1984: #**1** - 2 wks.

457.
I Wanna Dance With Somebody
(Who Loves Me)...
Whitney Houston
1987: #**1** - 2 wks.

458.
Gypsys, Tramps & Thieves...
Cher
1971: #**1** - 2 wks.

459.
Tragedy...
Bee Gees
1979: #**1** - 2 wks.

460.
Love Hangover...
Diana Ross
1976: #**1** - 2 wks.

461.
Sleep Walk...
Santo & Johnny
1959: #**1** - 2 wks.

462.
Calcutta...
Lawrence Welk
1961: #**1** - 2 wks.

463.
You've Lost That Lovin' Feelin'...
The Righteous Brothers
1965: #**1** - 2 wks.

464.
That's The Way (I Like It)...
KC And The Sunshine Band
1975: #**1** - 2 wks.

465.
I Get Around...
The Beach Boys
1964: #**1** - 2 wks.

466.
Just My Imagination (Running
Away With Me)...
The Temptations
1971: #**1** - 2 wks.

467.
Downtown...
Petula Clark
1965: #**1** - 2 wks.

468.
Johnny Angel...
Shelley Fabares
1962: #**1** - 2 wks.

TOP 1000 — 1955-2005

469.
Mama Told Me (Not To Come)...
Three Dog Night
1970: #**1** - 2 wks.

470.
Tighten Up...
Archie Bell & The Drells
1968: #**1** - 2 wks.

471.
No More Tears
(Enough Is Enough)...
Barbra Streisand/Donna Summer
1979: #**1** - 2 wks.

472.
Come See About Me...
The Supremes
1964: #**1** - 2 wks.

473.
Where Did Our Love Go...
The Supremes
1964: #**1** - 2 wks.

474.
Go Away Little Girl...
Steve Lawrence
1963: #**1** - 2 wks.

475.
Runaround Sue...
Dion
1961: #**1** - 2 wks.

476.
ABC...
The Jackson 5
1970: #**1** - 2 wks.

477.
The Love You Save...
The Jackson 5
1970: #**1** - 2 wks.

TOP 1000 — 1955-2005

478.
Theme From Shaft...
Isaac Hayes
1971: #**1** - 2 wks.

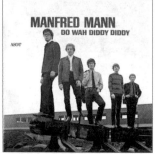

479.
Do Wah Diddy Diddy...
Manfred Mann
1964: #**1** - 2 wks.

480.
Michael...
The Highwaymen
1961: #**1** - 2 wks.

481.
This Diamond Ring...
Gary Lewis And The Playboys
1965: #**1** - 2 wks.

482.
Hello, I Love You...
The Doors
1968: #**1** - 2 wks.

483.
The First Time...
Surface
1991: #**1** - 2 wks.

484.
Butterfly...
Crazy Town
2001: #**1** - 2 wks.

485.
Look Away...
Chicago
1988: #**1** - 2 wks.

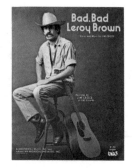

486.
Bad, Bad Leroy Brown...
Jim Croce
1973: #**1** - 2 wks.

487.
I Want To Know What Love Is...
Foreigner
1985: #**1** - 2 wks.

488.
My Heart Will Go On
(Love Theme From 'Titanic')...
Celine Dion
1998: #**1** - 2 wks.

489.
Top Of The World...
Carpenters
1973: #**1** - 2 wks.

490.
Midnight Train To Georgia...
Gladys Knight and The Pips
1973: #**1** - 2 wks.

491.
Everybody's Somebody's Fool...
Connie Francis
1960: #**1** - 2 wks.

492.
Grease...
Frankie Valli
1978: #**1** - 2 wks.

493.
Nothing's Gonna Stop Us Now...
Starship
1987: #**1** - 2 wks.

494.
The Reflex...
Duran Duran
1984: #**1** - 2 wks.

495.
The Power Of Love...
Huey Lewis And The News
1985: #**1** - 2 wks.

TOP 1000 — 1955-2005

496.
We Didn't Start The Fire...
Billy Joel
1989: #**1** - 2 wks.

497.
Brother Louie...
Stories
1973: #**1** - 2 wks.

498.
Travelin' Man...
Ricky Nelson
1961: #**1** - 2 wks.

499.
Everybody Wants To
Rule The World...
Tears For Fears
1985: #**1** - 2 wks.

500.
Will It Go Round In Circles...
Billy Preston
1973: #**1** - 2 wks.

501.
Heartbreaker...
Mariah Carey (Featuring Jay-Z)
1999: #**1** - 2 wks.

502.
Half-Breed...
Cher
1973: #**1** - 2 wks.

503.
I'll Be There...
Mariah Carey
1992: #**1** - 2 wks.

504.
Rapture...
Blondie
1981: #**1** - 2 wks.

505.
Afternoon Delight...
Starland Vocal Band
1976: #**1** - 2 wks.

506.
I Don't Wanna Cry...
Mariah Carey
1991: #**1** - 2 wks.

507.
Butterfly...
Charlie Gracie
1957: #**1** - 2 wks.

508.
Na Na Hey Hey Kiss Him Goodbye...
Steam
1969: #**1** - 2 wks.

509.
Judy In Disguise (With Glasses)...
John Fred & His Playboy Band
1968: #**1** - 2 wks.

510.
Justify My Love...
Madonna
1991: #**1** - 2 wks.

511.
My Guy...
Mary Wells
1964: #**1** - 2 wks.

512.
Get A Job...
The Silhouettes
1958: #**1** - 2 wks.

513.
With A Little Luck...
Wings
1978: #**1** - 2 wks.

TOP 1000 — 1955-2005

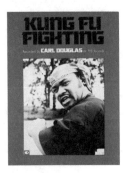

514.
Kung Fu Fighting...
Carl Douglas
1974: #**1** - 2 wks.

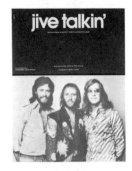

515.
Jive Talkin'...
Bee Gees
1975: #**1** - 2 wks.

516.
Kansas City...
Wilbert Harrison
1959: #**1** - 2 wks.

517.
Me And Bobby McGee...
Janis Joplin
1971: #**1** - 2 wks.

518.
Quarter To Three...
U.S. Bonds
1961: #**1** - 2 wks.

519.
Love Theme From Romeo & Juliet...
Henry Mancini
1969: #**1** - 2 wks.

520.
A Hard Day's Night...
The Beatles
1964: #**1** - 2 wks.

521.
Brown Sugar...
The Rolling Stones
1971: #**1** - 2 wks.

522.
Hit The Road Jack...
Ray Charles
1961: #**1** - 2 wks.

523.
You Can't Hurry Love...
The Supremes
1966: #**1** - 2 wks.

524.
Surrender...
Elvis Presley
1961: #**1** - 2 wks.

525.
Stop! In The Name Of Love...
The Supremes
1965: #**1** - 2 wks.

526.
Wild Thing...
The Troggs
1966: #**1** - 2 wks.

527.
Celebration...
Kool & The Gang
1981: #**1** - 2 wks.

528.
What A Girl Wants...
Christina Aguilera
2000: #**1** - 2 wks.

529.
Baby Baby...
Amy Grant
1991: #**1** - 2 wks.

530.
Cream...
Prince And The N.P.G.
1991: #**1** - 2 wks.

531.
Caribbean Queen (No More
Love On The Run)...
Billy Ocean
1984: #**1** - 2 wks.

532.
We Built This City...
Starship
1985: #**1** - 2 wks.

533.
Black Velvet...
Alannah Myles
1990: #**1** - 2 wks.

534.
All The Man That I Need...
Whitney Houston
1991: #**1** - 2 wks.

535.
Release Me...
Wilson Phillips
1990: #**1** - 2 wks.

536.
Will You Love Me Tomorrow...
The Shirelles
1961: #**1** - 2 wks.

537.
Someday...
Mariah Carey
1991: #**1** - 2 wks.

538.
Never Gonna Give You Up...
Rick Astley
1988: #**1** - 2 wks.

539.
Sweet Child O' Mine...
Guns N' Roses
1988: #**1** - 2 wks.

540.
Anything For You...
*Gloria Estefan and Miami
Sound Machine*
1988: #**1** - 2 wks.

541.
St. Elmo's Fire (Man In Motion)...
John Parr
1985: #**1** - 2 wks.

542.
I Adore Mi Amor...
Color Me Badd
1991: #**1** - 2 wks.

543.
The Night The Lights Went
Out In Georgia...
Vicki Lawrence
1973: #**1** - 2 wks.

544.
Get Outta My Dreams,
Get Into My Car...
Billy Ocean
1988: #**1** - 2 wks.

545.
Coming Out Of The Dark...
Gloria Estefan
1991: #**1** - 2 wks.

546.
She Ain't Worth It...
*Glenn Medeiros (Featuring
Bobby Brown)*
1990: #**1** - 2 wks.

547.
Kyrie...
Mr. Mister
1986: #**1** - 2 wks.

548.
Kiss...
Prince And The Revolution
1986: #**1** - 2 wks.

549.
Papa Don't Preach...
Madonna
1986: #**1** - 2 wks.

550.
Two Hearts...
Phil Collins
1989: #1 - 2 wks.

551.
I Still Haven't Found What
I'm Looking For...
U2
1987: #1 - 2 wks.

552.
Man In The Mirror...
Michael Jackson
1988: #1 - 2 wks.

553.
Didn't We Almost Have It All...
Whitney Houston
1987: #1 - 2 wks.

554.
Billy, Don't Be A Hero...
Bo Donaldson And The Heywoods
1974: #1 - 2 wks.

555.
He's A Rebel...
The Crystals
1962: #1 - 2 wks.

556.
I Knew You Were Waiting (For Me)...
Aretha Franklin & George Michael
1987: #1 - 2 wks.

557.
Time In A Bottle...
Jim Croce
1973: #1 - 2 wks.

558.
Reach Out I'll Be There...
Four Tops
1966: #1 - 2 wks.

559.
I'm Leaving It Up To You...
Dale & Grace
1963: #**1** - 2 wks.

560.
Breaking Up Is Hard To Do...
Neil Sedaka
1962: #**1** - 2 wks.

561.
Monster Mash...
Bobby "Boris" Pickett
1962: #**1** - 2 wks.

562.
Thank You (Falettinme
Be Mice Elf Agin)...
Sly & The Family Stone
1970: #**1** - 2 wks.

563.
A Moment Like This...
Kelly Clarkson
2002: #**1** - 2 wks.

564.
Annie's Song...
John Denver
1974: #**1** - 2 wks.

565.
Help Me, Rhonda...
The Beach Boys
1965: #**1** - 2 wks.

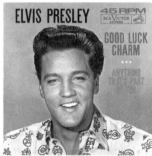

566.
Good Luck Charm...
Elvis Presley
1962: #**1** - 2 wks.

567.
Surf City...
Jan & Dean
1963: #**1** - 2 wks.

568.
It's My Party...
Lesley Gore
1963: #**1** - 2 wks.

569.
Walk Right In...
The Rooftop Singers
1963: #**1** - 2 wks.

570.
Rag Doll...
The 4 Seasons
1964: #**1** - 2 wks.

571.
Respect...
Aretha Franklin
1967: #**1** - 2 wks.

572.
A Big Hunk O' Love...
Elvis Presley
1959: #**1** - 2 wks.

573.
Easier Said Than Done...
The Essex
1963: #**1** - 2 wks.

574.
Kind Of A Drag...
The Buckinghams
1967: #**1** - 2 wks.

575.
Grazing In The Grass...
Hugh Masekela
1968: #**1** - 2 wks.

576.
Paint It, Black...
The Rolling Stones
1966: #**1** - 2 wks.

577.
The Most Beautiful Girl...
Charlie Rich
1973: #**1** - 2 wks.

578.
How Will I Know...
Whitney Houston
1986: #**1** - 2 wks.

579.
Bailamos...
Enrique Iglesias
1999: #**1** - 2 wks.

580.
When I See You Smile...
Bad English
1989: #**1** - 2 wks.

581.
Morning Train (Nine To Five)...
Sheena Easton
1981: #**1** - 2 wks.

582.
At This Moment...
Billy Vera & The Beaters
1987: #**1** - 2 wks.

583.
The Flame...
Cheap Trick
1988: #**1** - 2 wks.

584.
Blame It On The Rain...
Milli Vanilli
1989: #**1** - 2 wks.

585.
Forever Your Girl...
Paula Abdul
1989: #**1** - 2 wks.

586.
Girl I'm Gonna Miss You...
Milli Vanilli
1989: #**1** - 2 wks.

587.
Glory Of Love...
Peter Cetera
1986: #**1** - 2 wks.

588.
Fame...
David Bowie
1975: #**1** - 2 wks.

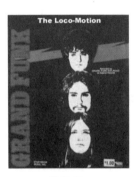

589.
The Loco-Motion...
Grand Funk
1974: #**1** - 2 wks.

590.
Could've Been...
Tiffany
1988: #**1** - 2 wks.

591.
Everything She Wants...
Wham!
1985: #**1** - 2 wks.

592.
Rich Girl...
Daryl Hall & John Oates
1977: #**1** - 2 wks.

593.
Heaven...
Bryan Adams
1985: #**1** - 2 wks.

594.
TSOP (The Sound Of Philadelphia)...
MFSB featuring The Three Degrees
1974: #**1** - 2 wks.

595.
Hard Headed Woman...
Elvis Presley
1958: #**1** - 2 wks.

596.
Don't Worry Be Happy...
Bobby McFerrin
1988: #**1** - 2 wks.

597.
Groovy Kind Of Love...
Phil Collins
1988: #**1** - 2 wks.

598.
I Think We're Alone Now...
Tiffany
1987: #**1** - 2 wks.

599.
Toy Soldiers...
Martika
1989: #**1** - 2 wks.

600.
Star Wars Theme/Cantina Band...
Meco
1977: #**1** - 2 wks.

601.
When I Think Of You...
Janet Jackson
1986: #**1** - 2 wks.

602.
(I Just) Died In Your Arms...
Cutting Crew
1987: #**1** - 2 wks.

603.
Where Do Broken Hearts Go...
Whitney Houston
1988: #**1** - 2 wks.

604.
A View To A Kill...
Duran Duran
1985: #**1** - 2 wks.

605.
Father Figure...
George Michael
1988: #**1** - 2 wks.

606.
Everything Is Beautiful...
Ray Stevens
1970: #**1** - 2 wks.

607.
Bad Medicine...
Bon Jovi
1988: #**1** - 2 wks.

608.
True Colors...
Cyndi Lauper
1986: #**1** - 2 wks.

609.
Bootylicious...
Destiny's Child
2001: #**1** - 2 wks.

610.
One More Night...
Phil Collins
1985: #**1** - 2 wks.

611.
Amanda...
Boston
1986: #**1** - 2 wks.

612.
I Can Help...
Billy Swan
1974: #**1** - 2 wks.

613.
Lean On Me...
Club Nouveau
1987: #**1** - 2 wks.

614.
My Ding-A-Ling...
Chuck Berry
1972: #**1** - 2 wks.

615.
Monkey...
George Michael
1988: #**1** - 2 wks.

616.
The Morning After...
Maureen McGovern
1973: #**1** - 2 wks.

617.
Sheila...
Tommy Roe
1962: #**1** - 2 wks.

618.
If You Wanna Be Happy...
Jimmy Soul
1963: #**1** - 2 wks.

619.
Get Off Of My Cloud...
The Rolling Stones
1965: #**1** - 2 wks.

620.
Lucy In The Sky With Diamonds...
Elton John
1975: #**1** - 2 wks.

621.
When A Man Loves A Woman...
Percy Sledge
1966: #**1** - 2 wks.

TOP 1000 — 1955-2005

622.
You Keep Me Hangin' On...
The Supremes
1966: #**1** - 2 wks.

623.
Hanky Panky...
Tommy James & The Shondells
1966: #**1** - 2 wks.

624.
The Long And Winding Road...
The Beatles
1970: #**1** - 2 wks.

625.
I Hear A Symphony...
The Supremes
1965: #**1** - 2 wks.

626.
My Love...
Petula Clark
1966: #**1** - 2 wks.

627.
I'm Telling You Now...
Freddie & The Dreamers
1965: #**1** - 2 wks.

628.
The Sounds Of Silence...
Simon & Garfunkel
1966: #**1** - 2 wks.

629.
Bad...
Michael Jackson
1987: #**1** - 2 wks.

630.
Rock Your Baby...
George McCrae
1974: #**1** - 2 wks.

TOP 1000 — 1955-2005

631.
I Honestly Love You...
Olivia Newton-John
1974: #**1** - 2 wks.

632.
Paperback Writer...
The Beatles
1966: #**1** - 2 wks.

633.
Eight Days A Week...
The Beatles
1965: #**1** - 2 wks.

634.
This Is The Night...
Clay Aiken
2003: #**1** - 2 wks.

635.
The Way You Move...
OutKast Featuring Sleepy Brown
2004: #**1** - 1 wks.

636.
You're Makin' Me High...
Toni Braxton
1996: #**1** - 1 wks.

637.
Everything You Want...
Vertical Horizon
2000: #**1** - 1 wks.

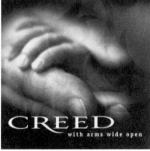

638.
With Arms Wide Open...
Creed
2000: #**1** - 1 wks.

639.
Kiss From A Rose...
Seal
1995: #**1** - 1 wks.

640.
Stand Up...
Ludacris
2003: #**1** - 1 wks.

641.
Try Again...
Aaliyah
2000: #**1** - 1 wks.

642.
Exhale (Shoop Shoop)...
Whitney Houston
1995: #**1** - 1 wks.

643.
Patricia...
Perez Prado
1958: #**1** - 1 wks.

644.
Bent...
Matchbox Twenty
2000: #**1** - 1 wks.

645.
All 4 Love...
Color Me Badd
1992: #**1** - 1 wks.

646.
Lately...
Divine
1998: #**1** - 1 wks.

647.
Angel...
Shaggy Featuring Rayvon
2001: #**1** - 1 wks.

648.
Do That To Me One More Time...
The Captain & Tennille
1980: #**1** - 1 wks.

649.
Hot Diggity...
Perry Como
1956: #**1** - 1 wks.

650.
Chances Are...
Johnny Mathis
1957: #**1** - 1 wks.

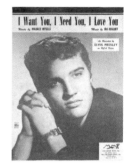

651.
I Want You, I Need You,
I Love You...
Elvis Presley
1956: #**1** - 1 wks.

652.
Slow Jamz...
*Twista Featuring Kanye West
& Jamie Foxx*
2004: #**1** - 1 wks.

653.
Hello, Dolly!...
Louis Armstrong
1964: #**1** - 1 wks.

654.
Don't Forbid Me...
Pat Boone
1957: #**1** - 1 wks.

655.
Young Love...
Sonny James
1957: #**1** - 1 wks.

656.
Still...
Commodores
1979: #**1** - 1 wks.

657.
Ms. Jackson...
OutKast
2001: #**1** - 1 wks.

658.
Diana...
Paul Anka
1957: #**1** - 1 wks.

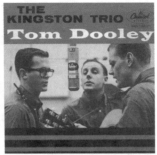

659.
Tom Dooley...
The Kingston Trio
1958: #**1** - 1 wks.

660.
My All...
Mariah Carey
1998: #**1** - 1 wks.

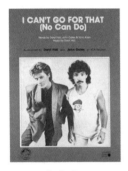

661.
I Can't Go For That (No Can Do)...
Daryl Hall & John Oates
1982: #**1** - 1 wks.

662.
Catch A Falling Star...
Perry Como
1958: #**1** - 1 wks.

663.
Twilight Time...
The Platters
1958: #**1** - 1 wks.

664.
Bump, Bump, Bump...
B2K & P. Diddy
2003: #**1** - 1 wks.

665.
Please Don't Go...
K.C. & The Sunshine Band
1980: #**1** - 1 wks.

666.
Mr. Blue...
The Fleetwoods
1959: #**1** - 1 wks.

667.
(Shake, Shake, Shake) Shake
Your Booty...
KC And The Sunshine Band
1976: #**1** - 1 wks.

668.
Little Star...
The Elegants
1958: #**1** - 1 wks.

669.
Stranger On The Shore...
Mr. Acker Bilk
1962: #**1** - 1 wks.

670.
Bird Dog...
The Everly Brothers
1958: #**1** - 1 wks.

671.
A Fifth Of Beethoven...
Walter Murphy/Big Apple Band
1976: #**1** - 1 wks.

672.
4 Seasons Of Loneliness...
Boyz II Men
1997: #**1** - 1 wks.

673.
Mickey...
Toni Basil
1982: #**1** - 1 wks.

674.
A Whole New World
(Aladdin's Theme)...
Peabo Bryson and Regina Belle
1993: #**1** - 1 wks.

675.
The Tide Is High...
Blondie
1981: #**1** - 1 wks.

676.
Disco Duck (Part I)...
Rick Dees
1976: #**1** - 1 wks.

677.
If I Can't Have You...
Yvonne Elliman
1978: #**1** - 1 wks.

678.
Bills, Bills, Bills...
Destiny's Child
1999: #**1** - 1 wks.

679.
I Write The Songs...
Barry Manilow
1976: #**1** - 1 wks.

680.
Party Doll...
Buddy Knox/The Rhythm Orchids
1957: #**1** - 1 wks.

681.
Leaving On A Jet Plane...
Peter, Paul And Mary
1969: #**1** - 1 wks.

682.
You Are Not Alone...
Michael Jackson
1995: #**1** - 1 wks.

683.
Let's Dance...
David Bowie
1983: #**1** - 1 wks.

684.
One Of These Nights...
Eagles
1975: #**1** - 1 wks.

685.
Brandy (You're A Fine Girl)...
Looking Glass
1972: #**1** - 1 wks.

686.
Love Rollercoaster...
Ohio Players
1976: #**1** - 1 wks.

687.
Make It With You...
Bread
1970: #**1** - 1 wks.

688.
Keep On Loving You...
REO Speedwagon
1981: #**1** - 1 wks.

689.
Pop Muzik...
M
1979: #**1** - 1 wks.

690.
Sad Eyes...
Robert John
1979: #**1** - 1 wks.

691.
Hot Child In The City...
Nick Gilder
1978: #**1** - 1 wks.

692.
Hold On...
Wilson Phillips
1990: #**1** - 1 wks.

693.
Who Can It Be Now?...
Men At Work
1982: #**1** - 1 wks.

TOP 1000 — 1955-2005

694.
Sweet Dreams (Are Made of This)...
Eurythmics
1983: #**1** - 1 wks.

695.
More Than Words...
Extreme
1991: #**1** - 1 wks.

696.
I Like The Way (The Kissing Game)...
Hi-Five
1991: #**1** - 1 wks.

697.
One More Try...
Timmy -T-
1991: #**1** - 1 wks.

698.
You're The One That I Want...
John Travolta & Olivia Newton-John
1978: #**1** - 1 wks.

699.
Missing You...
John Waite
1984: #**1** - 1 wks.

700.
Unbelievable...
EMF
1991: #**1** - 1 wks.

701.
That'll Be The Day...
The Crickets
1957: #**1** - 1 wks.

702.
Separate Lives...
Phil Collins & Marilyn Martin
1985: #**1** - 1 wks.

703.
When A Man Loves A Woman...
Michael Bolton
1991: **#1** - 1 wks.

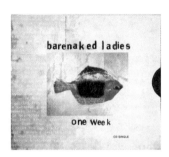

704.
One Week...
Barenaked Ladies
1998: **#1** - 1 wks.

705.
Miss You...
The Rolling Stones
1978: **#1** - 1 wks.

706.
I Want You Back...
The Jackson 5
1970: **#1** - 1 wks.

707.
Bennie And The Jets...
Elton John
1974: **#1** - 1 wks.

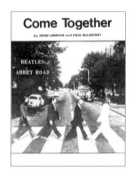

708.
Come Together...
The Beatles
1969: **#1** - 1 wks.

709.
Chariots Of Fire...
Vangelis
1982: **#1** - 1 wks.

710.
Indian Reservation...
The Raiders
1971: **#1** - 1 wks.

711.
Got To Give It Up (Pt. I)...
Marvin Gaye
1977: **#1** - 1 wks.

712.
Someday We'll Be Together...
Diana Ross & The Supremes
1969: #**1** - 1 wks.

713.
Let's Stay Together...
Al Green
1972: #**1** - 1 wks.

714.
Yakety Yak...
The Coasters
1958: #**1** - 1 wks.

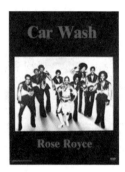

715.
Car Wash...
Rose Royce
1977: #**1** - 1 wks.

716.
Crazy For You...
Madonna
1985: #**1** - 1 wks.

717.
What A Fool Believes...
The Doobie Brothers
1979: #**1** - 1 wks.

718.
Good Times...
Chic
1979: #**1** - 1 wks.

719.
Incense And Peppermints...
Strawberry Alarm Clock
1967: #**1** - 1 wks.

720.
Mr. Lonely...
Bobby Vinton
1964: #**1** - 1 wks.

721.
The Stripper...
David Rose
1962: #**1** - 1 wks.

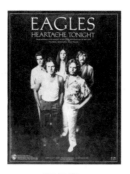

722.
Heartache Tonight...
Eagles
1979: #**1** - 1 wks.

723.
Venus...
The Shocking Blue
1970: #**1** - 1 wks.

724.
Why...
Frankie Avalon
1959: #**1** - 1 wks.

725.
96 Tears...
Question Mark & The Mysterians
1966: #**1** - 1 wks.

726.
Last Train To Clarksville...
The Monkees
1966: #**1** - 1 wks.

727.
Harper Valley P.T.A....
Jeannie C. Riley
1968: #**1** - 1 wks.

728.
You Don't Have To Be A Star
(To Be In My Show)...
Marilyn McCoo & Billy Davis, Jr.
1977: #**1** - 1 wks.

729.
Set Adrift On Memory Bliss...
PM Dawn
1991: #**1** - 1 wks.

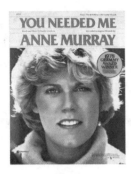

730.
You Needed Me...
Anne Murray
1978: #**1** - 1 wks.

731.
Need You Tonight...
INXS
1988: #**1** - 1 wks.

732.
Don't Leave Me This Way...
Thelma Houston
1977: #**1** - 1 wks.

733.
You Make Me Feel Like Dancing...
Leo Sayer
1977: #**1** - 1 wks.

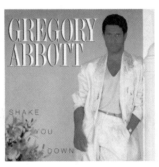

734.
Shake You Down...
Gregory Abbott
1987: #**1** - 1 wks.

735.
Touch Me In The Morning...
Diana Ross
1973: #**1** - 1 wks.

736.
Don't Let The Sun Go
Down On Me...
George Michael/Elton John
1992: #**1** - 1 wks.

737.
The Joker...
Steve Miller Band
1974: #**1** - 1 wks.

738.
Everytime You Go Away...
Paul Young
1985: #**1** - 1 wks.

739.
Dancing Queen...
Abba
1977: #**1** - 1 wks.

740.
The Way It Is...
Bruce Hornsby And The Range
1986: #**1** - 1 wks.

741.
Got My Mind Set On You...
George Harrison
1988: #**1** - 1 wks.

742.
Cold Hearted...
Paula Abdul
1989: #**1** - 1 wks.

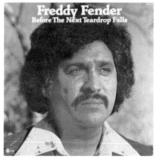

743.
Before The Next Teardrop Falls...
Freddy Fender
1975: #**1** - 1 wks.

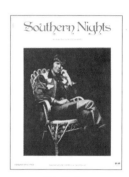

744.
Southern Nights...
Glen Campbell
1977: #**1** - 1 wks.

745.
Blinded By The Light...
Manfred Mann's Earth Band
1977: #**1** - 1 wks.

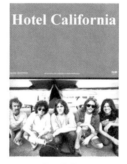

746.
Hotel California...
Eagles
1977: #**1** - 1 wks.

747.
Then Came You...
Dionne Warwicke & Spinners
1974: #**1** - 1 wks.

TOP 1000 — 1955-2005

TOP 1000 — 1955-2005

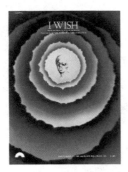

748.
I Wish...
Stevie Wonder
1977: #**1** - 1 wks.

749.
My Eyes Adored You...
Frankie Valli
1975: #**1** - 1 wks.

750.
Don't You (Forget About Me)...
Simple Minds
1985: #**1** - 1 wks.

751.
I Am Woman...
Helen Reddy
1972: #**1** - 1 wks.

752.
Medley...
Stars on 45
1981: #**1** - 1 wks.

753.
Part-Time Lover...
Stevie Wonder
1985: #**1** - 1 wks.

754.
Blaze Of Glory...
Jon Bon Jovi
1990: #**1** - 1 wks.

755.
This Used To Be My Playground...
Madonna
1992: #**1** - 1 wks.

756.
Delta Dawn...
Helen Reddy
1973: #**1** - 1 wks.

757.
I'm Your Baby Tonight...
Whitney Houston
1990: #**1** - 1 wks.

758.
So Emotional...
Whitney Houston
1988: #**1** - 1 wks.

759.
The One That You Love...
Air Supply
1981: #**1** - 1 wks.

760.
I'll Take You There...
The Staple Singers
1972: #**1** - 1 wks.

761.
Gonna Fly Now...
Bill Conti
1977: #**1** - 1 wks.

762.
Don't Wanna Lose You...
Gloria Estefan
1989: #**1** - 1 wks.

763.
Lovin' You...
Minnie Riperton
1975: #**1** - 1 wks.

764.
Want Ads...
The Honey Cone
1971: #**1** - 1 wks.

765.
Everybody Loves Somebody...
Dean Martin
1964: #**1** - 1 wks.

766.
Itsy Bitsy Teenie Weenie Yellow
Polkadot Bikini...
Brian Hyland
1960: #**1** - 1 wks.

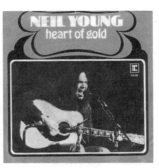

767.
Heart Of Gold...
Neil Young
1972: #**1** - 1 wks.

768.
Alley-Oop...
Hollywood Argyles
1960: #**1** - 1 wks.

769.
Mother-In-Law...
Ernie K-Doe
1961: #**1** - 1 wks.

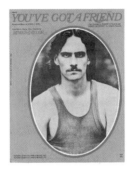

770.
You've Got A Friend...
James Taylor
1971: #**1** - 1 wks.

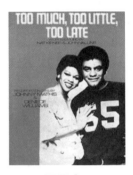

771.
Too Much, Too Little, Too Late...
Johnny Mathis/Deniece Williams
1978: #**1** - 1 wks.

772.
My Girl...
The Temptations
1965: #**1** - 1 wks.

773.
A World Without Love...
Peter And Gordon
1964: #**1** - 1 wks.

774.
Romantic...
Karyn White
1991: #**1** - 1 wks.

775.
Close To You...
Maxi Priest
1990: #**1** - 1 wks.

776.
Undercover Angel...
Alan O'Day
1977: #**1** - 1 wks.

777.
Wild, Wild West...
The Escape Club
1988: #**1** - 1 wks.

778.
Love's Theme...
Love Unlimited Orchestra
1974: #**1** - 1 wks.

779.
Show And Tell...
Al Wilson
1974: #**1** - 1 wks.

780.
Wind Beneath My Wings...
Bette Midler
1989: #**1** - 1 wks.

781.
Take On Me...
A-Ha
1985: #**1** - 1 wks.

782.
I Don't Have The Heart...
James Ingram
1990: #**1** - 1 wks.

783.
My Prerogative...
Bobby Brown
1989: #**1** - 1 wks.

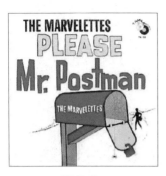

784.
Please Mr. Postman...
The Marvelettes
1961: #**1** - 1 wks.

785.
Love Will Never Do (Without You)...
Janet Jackson
1991: #**1** - 1 wks.

786.
Saving All My Love For You...
Whitney Houston
1985: #**1** - 1 wks.

787.
Ice Ice Baby...
Vanilla Ice
1990: #**1** - 1 wks.

788.
Boogie Fever...
Sylvers
1976: #**1** - 1 wks.

789.
Good Vibrations...
Marky Mark/Loleatta Holloway
1991: #**1** - 1 wks.

790.
Human...
Human League
1986: #**1** - 1 wks.

791.
Laughter In The Rain...
Neil Sedaka
1975: #**1** - 1 wks.

792.
Tell Her About It...
Billy Joel
1983: #**1** - 1 wks.

793.
Here I Go Again...
Whitesnake
1987: #**1** - 1 wks.

794.
(Can't Live Without Your)
Love And Affection...
Nelson
1990: #**1** - 1 wks.

795.
She Drives Me Crazy...
Fine Young Cannibals
1989: #**1** - 1 wks.

796.
Addicted To Love...
Robert Palmer
1986: #**1** - 1 wks.

797.
Always...
Atlantic Starr
1987: #**1** - 1 wks.

798.
Heart Of Glass...
Blondie
1979: #**1** - 1 wks.

799.
There'll Be Sad Songs
(To Make You Cry)...
Billy Ocean
1986: #**1** - 1 wks.

800.
Sledgehammer...
Peter Gabriel
1986: #**1** - 1 wks.

801.
West End Girls...
Pet Shop Boys
1986: #**1** - 1 wks.

802.
When I Need You...
Leo Sayer
1977: #**1** - 1 wks.

803.
Head To Toe...
Lisa Lisa And Cult Jam
1987: #**1** - 1 wks.

804.
Frankenstein...
The Edgar Winter Group
1973: #**1** - 1 wks.

805.
You Haven't Done Nothin...
Stevie Wonder
1974: #**1** - 1 wks.

806.
You're In Love...
Wilson Phillips
1991: #**1** - 1 wks.

807.
Shakedown...
Bob Seger
1987: #**1** - 1 wks.

808.
Nothing From Nothing...
Billy Preston
1974: #**1** - 1 wks.

809.
Another Somebody Done
Somebody Wrong Song...
B.J. Thomas
1975: #**1** - 1 wks.

810.
The Happy Organ...
Dave 'Baby' Cortez
1959: #**1** - 1 wks.

811.
Hooked On A Feeling...
Blue Swede
1974: #**1** - 1 wks.

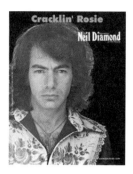

812.
Cracklin' Rosie...
Neil Diamond
1970: #**1** - 1 wks.

813.
Oh Girl...
Chi-Lites
1972: #**1** - 1 wks.

814.
Miami Vice Theme...
Jan Hammer
1985: #**1** - 1 wks.

815.
Take My Breath Away...
Berlin
1986: #**1** - 1 wks.

816.
Sailing...
Christopher Cross
1980: #**1** - 1 wks.

817.
If Wishes Came True...
Sweet Sensation
1990: #**1** - 1 wks.

818.
Sara...
Starship
1986: #**1** - 1 wks.

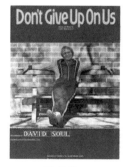

819.
Don't Give Up On Us...
David Soul
1977: #**1** - 1 wks.

820.
The Look...
Roxette
1989: #**1** - 1 wks.

821.
Dreams...
Fleetwood Mac
1977: #**1** - 1 wks.

822.
Sunshine On My Shoulders...
John Denver
1974: #**1** - 1 wks.

823.
Band On The Run...
Paul McCartney & Wings
1974: #**1** - 1 wks.

824.
Lady Marmalade...
LaBelle
1975: #**1** - 1 wks.

825.
You Are The Sunshine Of My Life...
Stevie Wonder
1973: #**1** - 1 wks.

826.
Pick Up The Pieces...
AWB
1975: #**1** - 1 wks.

827.
Theme From Mahogany (Do You
Know Where You're Going To)...
Diana Ross
1976: #**1** - 1 wks.

828.
Angie...
The Rolling Stones
1973: #**1** - 1 wks.

829.
New Kid In Town...
Eagles
1977: #**1** - 1 wks.

830.
Da Doo Ron Ron...
Shaun Cassidy
1977: #**1** - 1 wks.

831.
You Should Be Dancing...
Bee Gees
1976: #**1** - 1 wks.

832.
Venus...
Bananarama
1986: #**1** - 1 wks.

833.
Let Your Love Flow...
Bellamy Brothers
1976: #**1** - 1 wks.

834.
The Hustle...
Van McCoy
1975: #**1** - 1 wks.

835.
Black Water...
The Doobie Brothers
1975: #**1** - 1 wks.

836.
The Loco-Motion...
Little Eva
1962: #**1** - 1 wks.

837.
Wooden Heart...
Joe Dowell
1961: #**1** - 1 wks.

838.
You're Sixteen...
Ringo Starr
1974: #1 - 1 wks.

839.
Let's Do It Again...
The Staple Singers
1975: #1 - 1 wks.

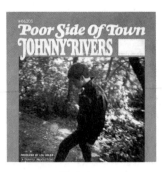

840.
Poor Side Of Town...
Johnny Rivers
1966: #1 - 1 wks.

841.
So Much In Love...
The Tymes
1963: #1 - 1 wks.

842.
Deep Purple...
Nino Tempo & April Stevens
1963: #1 - 1 wks.

843.
These Boots Are Made For Walkin'...
Nancy Sinatra
1966: #1 - 1 wks.

844.
Good Vibrations...
The Beach Boys
1966: #1 - 1 wks.

845.
Good Lovin'...
The Young Rascals
1966: #1 - 1 wks.

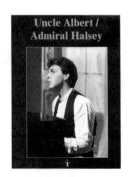

846.
Uncle Albert/Admiral Halsey...
Paul & Linda McCartney
1971: #1 - 1 wks.

TOP 1000 — 1955-2005

847.
Green Tambourine...
The Lemon Pipers
1968: #**1** - 1 wks.

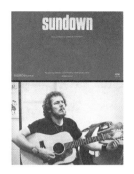

848.
Sundown...
Gordon Lightfoot
1974: #**1** - 1 wks.

849.
Ben...
Michael Jackson
1972: #**1** - 1 wks.

850.
Have You Never Been Mellow...
Olivia Newton-John
1975: #**1** - 1 wks.

851.
Convoy...
C.W. McCall
1976: #**1** - 1 wks.

852.
Strangers In The Night...
Frank Sinatra
1966: #**1** - 1 wks.

853.
Listen To What The Man Said...
Wings
1975: #**1** - 1 wks.

854.
Welcome Back...
John Sebastian
1976: #**1** - 1 wks.

855.
Give Me Love (Give Me
Peace On Earth)...
George Harrison
1973: #**1** - 1 wks.

103

TOP 1000 — 1955-2005

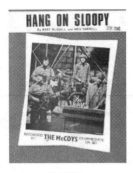

856.
Hang On Sloopy...
The McCoys
1965: #1 - 1 wks.

857.
Mr. Custer...
Larry Verne
1960: #1 - 1 wks.

858.
Sunshine Superman...
Donovan
1966: #1 - 1 wks.

859.
Mr. Tambourine Man...
The Byrds
1965: #1 - 1 wks.

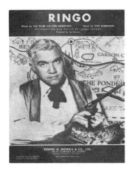

860.
Ringo...
Lorne Greene
1964: #1 - 1 wks.

861.
Love Is Here And Now
You're Gone...
The Supremes
1967: #1 - 1 wks.

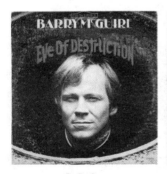

862.
Eve Of Destruction...
Barry McGuire
1965: #1 - 1 wks.

863.
Ruby Tuesday...
The Rolling Stones
1967: #1 - 1 wks.

864.
All You Need Is Love...
The Beatles
1967: #1 - 1 wks.

865.
Love Machine...
The Miracles
1976: #**1** - 1 wks.

866.
I'm Your Boogie Man...
KC And The Sunshine Band
1977: #**1** - 1 wks.

867.
Africa...
Toto
1983: #**1** - 1 wks.

868.
Seasons Change...
Exposé
1988: #**1** - 1 wks.

869.
Wishing Well...
Terence Trent D'Arby
1988: #**1** - 1 wks.

870.
Baby, I Love Your Way/
Freebird Medley (Free Baby)...
Will To Power
1988: #**1** - 1 wks.

871.
If You Don't Know Me By Now...
Simply Red
1989: #**1** - 1 wks.

872.
Heaven Is A Place On Earth...
Belinda Carlisle
1987: #**1** - 1 wks.

873.
(I've Had) The Time Of My Life...
Bill Medley & Jennifer Warnes
1987: #**1** - 1 wks.

874.
The Next Time I Fall...
Peter Cetera w/ Amy Grant
1986: #**1** - 1 wks.

875.
Love Will Lead You Back...
Taylor Dayne
1990: #**1** - 1 wks.

876.
You Give Love A Bad Name...
Bon Jovi
1986: #**1** - 1 wks.

877.
Come On Eileen...
Dexys Midnight Runners
1983: #**1** - 1 wks.

878.
Holding Back The Years...
Simply Red
1986: #**1** - 1 wks.

879.
Higher Love...
Steve Winwood
1986: #**1** - 1 wks.

880.
Listen To Your Heart...
Roxette
1989: #**1** - 1 wks.

881.
I'll Be Loving You (Forever)...
New Kids On The Block
1989: #**1** - 1 wks.

882.
Hold On To The Nights...
Richard Marx
1988: #**1** - 1 wks.

883.
Baby Don't Forget My Number...
Milli Vanilli
1989: #**1** - 1 wks.

884.
Knock On Wood...
Amii Stewart
1979: #**1** - 1 wks.

885.
The Living Years...
Mike & The Mechanics
1989: #**1** - 1 wks.

886.
Foolish Beat...
Debbie Gibson
1988: #**1** - 1 wks.

887.
Joyride...
Roxette
1991: #**1** - 1 wks.

888.
I've Been Thinking About You...
Londonbeat
1991: #**1** - 1 wks.

889.
Best Of My Love...
The Eagles
1975: #**1** - 1 wks.

890.
Eternal Flame...
Bangles
1989: #**1** - 1 wks.

891.
Open Your Heart...
Madonna
1987: #**1** - 1 wks.

892.
Wild Wild West...
Will Smith
1999: #**1** - 1 wks.

893.
Sussudio...
Phil Collins
1985: #**1** - 1 wks.

894.
Love Bites...
Def Leppard
1988: #**1** - 1 wks.

895.
I'll Be There For You...
Bon Jovi
1989: #**1** - 1 wks.

896.
Oh Sheila...
Ready For The World
1985: #**1** - 1 wks.

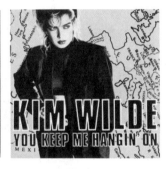

897.
You Keep Me Hangin' On...
Kim Wilde
1987: #**1** - 1 wks.

898.
These Dreams...
Heart
1986: #**1** - 1 wks.

899.
Lost In Emotion...
Lisa Lisa And Cult Jam
1987: #**1** - 1 wks.

900.
Rock Me Gently...
Andy Kim
1974: #**1** - 1 wks.

TOP 1000 — 1955·2005

901.
Live To Tell...
Madonna
1986: #**1** - 1 wks.

902.
The Way You Make Me Feel...
Michael Jackson
1988: #**1** - 1 wks.

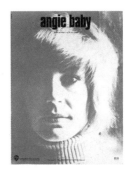

903.
Angie Baby...
Helen Reddy
1974: #**1** - 1 wks.

904.
We're An American Band...
Grand Funk
1973: #**1** - 1 wks.

905.
Good Thing...
Fine Young Cannibals
1989: #**1** - 1 wks.

906.
Superstition...
Stevie Wonder
1973: #**1** - 1 wks.

907.
Feel Like Makin' Love...
Roberta Flack
1974: #**1** - 1 wks.

908.
I Want To Be Wanted...
Brenda Lee
1960: #**1** - 1 wks.

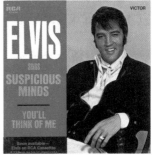

909.
Suspicious Minds...
Elvis Presley
1969: #**1** - 1 wks.

109

910.
Love Train...
O'Jays
1973: #**1** - 1 wks.

911.
Red Red Wine...
UB40
1988: #**1** - 1 wks.

912.
Theme From S.W.A.T....
Rhythm Heritage
1976: #**1** - 1 wks.

913.
Mony Mony "Live"...
Billy Idol
1987: #**1** - 1 wks.

914.
Don't Stop 'Til You Get Enough...
Michael Jackson
1979: #**1** - 1 wks.

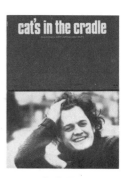

915.
Cat's In The Cradle...
Harry Chapin
1974: #**1** - 1 wks.

916.
Together Forever...
Rick Astley
1988: #**1** - 1 wks.

917.
Saturday Night...
Bay City Rollers
1976: #**1** - 1 wks.

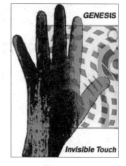

918.
Invisible Touch...
Genesis
1986: #**1** - 1 wks.

919.
Fallin' In Love...
Hamilton, Joe Frank And Reynolds
1975: #**1** - 1 wks.

920.
Hangin' Tough...
New Kids On The Block
1989: #**1** - 1 wks.

921.
Photograph...
Ringo Starr
1973: #**1** - 1 wks.

922.
Dark Lady...
Cher
1974: #**1** - 1 wks.

923.
Papa Was A Rollin' Stone...
The Temptations
1972: #**1** - 1 wks.

924.
Moody River...
Pat Boone
1961: #**1** - 1 wks.

925.
Jacob's Ladder...
Huey Lewis and the News
1987: #**1** - 1 wks.

926.
Song Sung Blue...
Neil Diamond
1972: #**1** - 1 wks.

927.
Batdance...
Prince
1989: #**1** - 1 wks.

928.
The Night Chicago Died...
Paper Lace
1974: #**1** - 1 wks.

929.
Who's That Girl...
Madonna
1987: #**1** - 1 wks.

930.
Love Me Do...
The Beatles
1964: #**1** - 1 wks.

931.
I Just Can't Stop Loving You...
Michael Jackson
1987: #**1** - 1 wks.

932.
Over And Over...
The Dave Clark Five
1965: #**1** - 1 wks.

933.
Lightnin' Strikes...
Lou Christie
1966: #**1** - 1 wks.

934.
Praying For Time...
George Michael
1990: #**1** - 1 wks.

935.
Our Day Will Come...
Ruby & The Romantics
1963: #**1** - 1 wks.

936.
Don't Break The Heart
That Loves You...
Connie Francis
1962: #**1** - 1 wks.

937.
The Happening...
The Supremes
1967: #**1** - 1 wks.

938.
Ticket To Ride...
The Beatles
1965: #**1** - 1 wks.

939.
I'm Henry VIII, I Am...
Herman's Hermits
1965: #**1** - 1 wks.

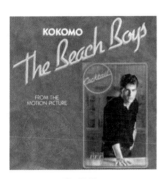

940.
Kokomo...
The Beach Boys
1988: #**1** - 1 wks.

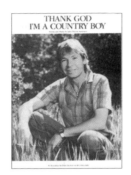

941.
Thank God I'm A Country Boy...
John Denver
1975: #**1** - 1 wks.

942.
Shining Star...
Earth, Wind & Fire
1975: #**1** - 1 wks.

943.
Rock'n Me...
Steve Miller
1976: #**1** - 1 wks.

944.
Stay...
Maurice Williams & The Zodiacs
1960: #**1** - 1 wks.

945.
When I'm With You...
Sheriff
1989: #**1** - 1 wks.

946.
Rock On...
Michael Damian
1989: #**1** - 1 wks.

947.
Looks Like We Made It...
Barry Manilow
1977: #**1** - 1 wks.

948.
Love You Inside Out...
Bee Gees
1979: #**1** - 1 wks.

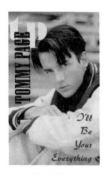

949.
I'll Be Your Everything...
Tommy Page
1990: #**1** - 1 wks.

950.
The Promise Of A New Day...
Paula Abdul
1991: #**1** - 1 wks.

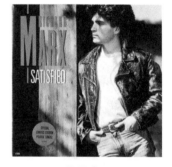

951.
Satisfied...
Richard Marx
1989: #**1** - 1 wks.

952.
You Ain't Seen Nothing Yet...
Bachman-Turner Overdrive
1974: #**1** - 1 wks.

953.
Please Mr. Postman...
Carpenters
1975: #**1** - 1 wks.

954.
Mandy...
Barry Manilow
1975: #**1** - 1 wks.

955.
Black Cat...
Janet Jackson
1990: #**1** - 1 wks.

956.
Dirty Diana...
Michael Jackson
1988: #**1** - 1 wks.

957.
Rock The Boat...
The Hues Corporation
1974: #**1** - 1 wks.

958.
You're No Good...
Linda Ronstadt
1975: #**1** - 1 wks.

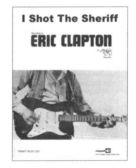

959.
I Shot The Sheriff...
Eric Clapton
1974: #**1** - 1 wks.

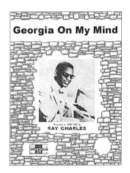

960.
Georgia On My Mind...
Ray Charles
1960: #**1** - 1 wks.

961.
Leader Of The Pack...
The Shangri-Las
1964: #**1** - 1 wks.

962.
Game Of Love...
Wayne Fontana & The Mindbenders
1965: #**1** - 1 wks.

963.
Back In My Arms Again...
The Supremes
1965: #**1** - 1 wks.

964.
Black & White...
Three Dog Night
1972: #**1** - 1 wks.

965.
Penny Lane...
The Beatles
1967: #**1** - 1 wks.

966.
Running Scared...
Roy Orbison
1961: #**1** - 1 wks.

967.
I'm Sorry...
John Denver
1975: #**1** - 1 wks.

968.
Fire...
Ohio Players
1975: #**1** - 1 wks.

969.
Sister Golden Hair...
America
1975: #**1** - 1 wks.

970.
Thank God I Found You...
Mariah With Joe & 98°
2000: #**1** - 1 wks.

971.
Get Down Tonight...
KC & The Sunshine Band
1975: #**1** - 1 wks.

972.
Can't Get Enough Of
Your Love, Babe...
Barry White
1974: #**1** - 1 wks.

973.
Inside Your Heaven...
Carrie Underwood
2005: #**1** - 1 wks.

974.
Whatever Gets You
Thru The Night...
John Lennon
1974: #**1** - 1 wks.

975.
I Believe...
Fantasia
2004: #**1** - 1 wks.

976.
Work It...
Missy "Misdemeanor" Elliott
2002: #**2** - 10 wks.

977.
Waiting For A Girl Like You...
Foreigner
1981: #**2** - 10 wks.

978.
You're Still The One...
Shania Twain
1998: #**2** - 9 wks.

979.
I Love You Always Forever...
Donna Lewis
1996: #**2** - 9 wks.

980.
Nobody's Supposed To Be Here...
Deborah Cox
1998: #**2** - 8 wks.

981.
Back At One...
Brian McKnight
1999: #**2** - 8 wks.

982.
If I Ever Fall In Love...
Shai
1992: #**2** - 8 wks.

983.
I Don't Wanna Know...
Mario Winans Feat. P. Diddy & Enya
2004: #**2** - 8 wks.

984.
Little Darlin'...
The Diamonds
1957: #**2** - 8 wks.

985.
Whoomp! (There It Is)...
Tag Team
1993: #**2** - 7 wks.

986.
You Make Me Wanna......
Usher
1997: #**2** - 7 wks.

987.
1,2 Step...
Ciara featuring Missy Elliott
2005: #**2** - 7 wks.

988.
What's Luv?...
Fat Joe Featuring Ashanti
2002: #**2** - 7 wks.

989.
Survivor...
Destiny's Child
2001: #**2** - 7 wks.

990.
Moments To Remember...
The Four Lads
1955: #**2** - 6 wks.

991.
All I Wanna Do...
Sheryl Crow
1994: #**2** - 6 wks.

992.
Baby-Baby-Baby...
TLC
1992: #**2** - 6 wks.

993.
Shake It Off...
Mariah Carey
2005: #**2** - 6 wks.

994.
Sometimes Love Just
Ain't Enough...
Patty Smyth with Don Henley
1992: #**2** - 6 wks.

995.
Open Arms...
Journey
1982: #**2** - 6 wks.

996.
Baker Street...
Gerry Rafferty
1978: #**2** - 6 wks.

997.
Louie Louie...
The Kingsmen
1963: #**2** - 6 wks.

998.
Breathe...
Faith Hill
2000: #**2** - 5 wks.

999.
It's All Coming Back To Me Now...
Celine Dion
1996: #**2** - 5 wks.

TOP 1000 — 1955-2005

1000.
Right Thurr...
Chingy
2003: #**2** - 5 wks.

1990s Airplay-Only Top Hits:

Iris...
Goo Goo Golls
1998: #**1**[A] - 18 wks.

Don't Speak...
No Doubt
1996: #**1**[A] - 16 wks.

Torn...
Natalie Imbruglia
1998: #**1**[A] - 11 wks.

Fly...
Sugar Ray
1997: #**1**[A] - 6 wks.

Men In Black...
Will Smith
1997: #**1**[A] - 4 wks.

Lovefool...
The Cardigans
1997: #**2**[A] - 8 wks.

One Headlight...
The Wallflowers
1997: #**2**[A] - 5 wks.

THE YEARS

This section lists each year's 40 biggest hits. These rankings are based on the Top 1000 ranking system.

You will find hundreds of additional hits in these yearly Top 40 rankings that do not appear in the Top 1000 ranking. A break separates Top 1000-ranked titles from those that do not rank within the Top 1000.

Columnar headings show the following data:

RANK: Top 1000 ranking
PEAK DATE: Date song reached its peak position
PEAK WKS: Total weeks song held its peak position
PEAK POS: Highest charted position song attained

RANK	PEAK DATE	PEAK WKS	PEAK POS		TITLE	ARTIST
35	7/9	8	1	1.	Rock Around The Clock	Bill Haley & His Comets
40	11/26	8	1	2.	Sixteen Tons	"Tennessee" Ernie Ford
78	10/8	6	1	3.	Love Is A Many-Splendored Thing	Four Aces
82	9/3	6	1	4.	The Yellow Rose Of Texas	Mitch Miller
157	10/29	4	1	5.	Autumn Leaves	Roger Williams
386	7/9	2	1	6.	Learnin' The Blues	Frank Sinatra
394	9/17	2	1	7.	Ain't That A Shame	Pat Boone
990	10/29	6	2	8.	Moments To Remember	The Four Lads
	12/10	3	2	9.	I Hear You Knocking	Gale Storm
	7/9	1	2	10.	A Blossom Fell	Nat "King" Cole
	11/26	2	3	11.	The Shifting, Whispering Sands	Rusty Draper
	9/17	1	3	12.	The Yellow Rose Of Texas	Johnny Desmond
	10/8	1	3	13.	Seventeen	The Fontane Sisters
	8/13	1	4	14.	Hard To Get	Gisele MacKenzie
	12/31	1	4	15.	He	Al Hibbler
	10/22	4	5	16.	The Shifting Whispering Sands Parts 1 & 2	Billy Vaughn
	11/5	3	5	17.	Only You (And You Alone)	The Platters
	11/26	3	5	18.	Love And Marriage	Frank Sinatra
	10/15	1	5	19.	Tina Marie	Perry Como
	7/23	1	5	20.	Something's Gotta Give	The McGuire Sisters
	9/10	1	5	21.	Maybellene	Chuck Berry

PRE-"ROCK AROUND THE CLOCK" HITS:

PEAK DATE	PEAK WKS	PEAK POS		TITLE	ARTIST
4/30	10	1	1.	Cherry Pink And Apple Blossom White	Perez Prado
2/12	10	1	2.	Sincerely	The McGuire Sisters
3/26	5	1	3.	The Ballad Of Davy Crockett	Bill Hayes
1/1	4	1	4.	Let Me Go Lover	Joan Weber
5/14	3	1	5.	Dance With Me Henry (Wallflower)	Georgia Gibbs
2/5	3	1	6.	Hearts Of Stone	The Fontane Sisters
5/14	2	1	7.	Unchained Melody	Les Baxter
3/12	7	2	8.	The Crazy Otto	Johnny Maddox
3/5	3	2	9.	Ko Ko Mo (I Love You So)	Perry Como
3/5	1	2	10.	Melody Of Love	Billy Vaughn
4/2	1	2	11.	Tweedle Dee	Georgia Gibbs
4/9	1	2	12.	How Important Can It Be?	Joni James
1/1	4	3	13.	The Naughty Lady Of Shady Lane	The Ames Brothers
6/4	1	3	14.	Unchained Melody	Al Hibbler
3/12	1	3	15.	Melody Of Love	Four Aces
2/26	1	3	16.	That's All I Want From You	Jaye P. Morgan
3/12	1	3	17.	Earth Angel	The Crew-Cuts
5/14	4	5	18.	Ballad Of Davy Crockett	"Tennessee" Ernie Ford
5/21	1	5	19.	Ballad Of Davy Crockett	Fess Parker

TOP 40 HITS   1956

RANK	PEAK DATE	PEAK WKS	PEAK POS		TITLE	ARTIST
13	8/18	11	1	1.	Don't Be Cruel / Hound Dog	Elvis Presley
20	12/8	10	1	2.	Singing The Blues	Guy Mitchell
39	6/16	8	1	3.	The Wayward Wind	Gogi Grant
41	4/21	8	1	4.	Heartbreak Hotel	Elvis Presley
80	2/18	6	1	5.	Rock And Roll Waltz	Kay Starr
81	3/17	6	1	6.	The Poor People Of Paris	Les Baxter
85	1/7	6	1	7.	Memories Are Made Of This	Dean Martin
113	11/3	5	1	8.	Love Me Tender	Elvis Presley
115	8/4	5	1	9.	My Prayer	The Platters
160	2/25	4	1	10.	Lisbon Antigua	Nelson Riddle
169	7/28	4	1	11.	I Almost Lost My Mind	Pat Boone
248	11/3	3	1	12.	The Green Door	Jim Lowe
254	6/2	3	1	13.	Moonglow and Theme From "Picnic"	Morris Stoloff
400	2/18	2	1	14.	The Great Pretender	The Platters
649	5/5	1	1	15.	Hot Diggity (Dog Ziggity Boom)	Perry Como
651	7/28	1	1	16.	I Want You, I Need You, I Love You	Elvis Presley
	3/17	4	2	17.	No, Not Much!	The Four Lads
	5/19	4	2	18.	Blue Suede Shoes	Carl Perkins
	10/6	3	2	19.	Honky Tonk (Parts 1 & 2)	Bill Doggett
	8/18	3	2	20.	Whatever Will Be, Will Be (Que Sera, Sera)	Doris Day
	10/13	2	2	21.	Canadian Sunset	Hugo Winterhalter/Eddie Heywood
	8/18	2	2	22.	Allegheny Moon	Patti Page
	10/27	1	2	23.	Just Walking In The Rain	Johnnie Ray
	6/16	1	2	24.	Ivory Tower	Cathy Carr
	6/16	3	3	25.	Standing On The Corner	The Four Lads
	7/14	2	3	26.	I'm In Love Again	Fats Domino
	11/10	1	3	27.	True Love	Bing Crosby & Grace Kelly
	8/25	1	3	28.	The Flying Saucer Parts 1 & 2	Buchanan & Goodman
	7/7	4	4	29.	On The Street Where You Live	Vic Damone
	5/19	3	4	30.	(You've Got) The Magic Touch	The Platters
	1/7	1	4	31.	Band Of Gold	Don Cherry
	4/7	1	4	32.	I'll Be Home	Pat Boone
	10/6	1	4	33.	Tonight You Belong To Me	Patience & Prudence
	6/2	1	4	34.	Moonglow And Theme From "Picnic"	George Cates
	7/21	1	4	35.	More	Perry Como
	5/12	2	5	36.	A Tear Fell	Teresa Brewer
	7/14	2	5	37.	Born To Be With You	The Chordettes
	10/20	1	5	38.	Friendly Persuasion (Thee I Love)	Pat Boone
	1/14	1	5	39.	Memories Are Made Of This	Gale Storm
	2/11	4	6	40.	See You Later, Alligator	Bill Haley & His Comets

TOP 40 HITS   1957

RANK	PEAK DATE	PEAK WKS	PEAK POS		TITLE	ARTIST
29	4/13	9	1	1.	All Shook Up	Elvis Presley
52	6/3	7	1	2.	Love Letters In The Sand	Pat Boone
55	10/21	7	1	3.	Jailhouse Rock	Elvis Presley
58	7/8	7	1	4.	Let Me Be Your Teddy Bear	Elvis Presley
88	12/16	6	1	5.	April Love	Pat Boone
92	2/16	6	1	6.	Young Love	Tab Hunter
109	8/19	5	1	7.	Tammy	Debbie Reynolds
171	9/23	4	1	8.	Honeycomb	Jimmie Rodgers
180	10/14	4	1	9.	Wake Up Little Susie	The Everly Brothers
261	12/2	3	1	10.	You Send Me	Sam Cooke
292	3/30	3	1	11.	Butterfly	Andy Williams
304	2/9	3	1	12.	Too Much	Elvis Presley
398	4/6	2	1	13.	Round And Round	Perry Como
507	4/13	2	1	14.	Butterfly	Charlie Gracie
650	10/21	1	1	15.	Chances Are	Johnny Mathis
654	2/9	1	1	16.	Don't Forbid Me	Pat Boone
655	2/9	1	1	17.	Young Love	Sonny James
658	9/9	1	1	18.	Diana	Paul Anka
680	3/30	1	1	19.	Party Doll	Buddy Knox
701	9/23	1	1	20.	That'll Be The Day	The Crickets
984	4/6	8	2	21.	Little Darlin'	The Diamonds
	6/17	4	2	22.	So Rare	Jimmy Dorsey
	6/17	4	2	23.	Bye Bye Love	The Everly Brothers
	1/19	3	2	24.	Blueberry Hill	Fats Domino
	1/5	2	2	25.	Love Me	Elvis Presley
	3/16	2	2	26.	Teen-Age Crush	Tommy Sands
	6/3	1	2	27.	A White Sport Coat (And A Pink Carnation)	Marty Robbins
	12/16	1	2	28.	Raunchy	Bill Justis
	6/10	1	2	29.	A Teenager's Romance	Ricky Nelson
	8/5	4	3	30.	I'm Gonna Sit Right Down And Write Myself A Letter	Billy Williams
	12/16	1	3	31.	Kisses Sweeter Than Wine	Jimmie Rodgers
	12/30	3	3	32.	Peggy Sue	Buddy Holly
	5/13	3	3	33.	School Day	Chuck Berry
	9/9	2	3	34.	Whole Lot Of Shakin' Going On	Jerry Lee Lewis
	11/4	2	3	35.	Silhouettes	The Rays
	7/29	1	3	36.	Searchin'	The Coasters
	7/29	1	3	37.	Old Cape Cod	Patti Page
	1/19	1	3	38.	Moonlight Gambler	Frankie Laine
	1/12	1	3	39.	Hey! Jealous Lover	Frank Sinatra
	4/6	1	3	40.	Marianne	The Hilltoppers

RANK	PEAK DATE	PEAK WKS	PEAK POS		TITLE	ARTIST
61	1/6	7	1	1.	At The Hop	Danny & The Juniors
95	9/29	6	1	2.	It's All In The Game	Tommy Edwards
103	6/9	6	1	3.	The Purple People Eater	Sheb Wooley
123	5/12	5	1	4.	All I Have To Do Is Dream	The Everly Brothers
126	3/17	5	1	5.	Tequila	The Champs
131	2/10	5	1	6.	Don't	Elvis Presley
139	8/18	5	1	7.	Nel Blu Dipinto Di Blu (Volaré)	Domenico Modugno
183	2/17	4	1	8.	Sugartime	The McGuire Sisters
218	4/14	4	1	9.	He's Got The Whole World (In His Hands)	Laurie London
244	12/22	4	1	10.	The Chipmunk Song	The Chipmunks
266	4/28	3	1	11.	Witch Doctor	David Seville
273	12/1	3	1	12.	To Know Him, Is To Love Him	The Teddy Bears
420	8/4	2	1	13.	Poor Little Fool	Ricky Nelson
427	11/10	2	1	14.	It's Only Make Believe	Conway Twitty
512	2/24	2	1	15.	Get A Job	The Silhouettes
595	7/21	2	1	16.	Hard Headed Woman	Elvis Presley
643	7/28	1	1	17.	Patricia	Perez Prado
659	11/17	1	1	18.	Tom Dooley	The Kingston Trio
662	3/24	1	1	19.	Catch A Falling Star	Perry Como
663	4/21	1	1	20.	Twilight Time	The Platters
668	8/25	1	1	21.	Little Star	The Elegants
670	8/25	1	1	22.	Bird Dog	The Everly Brothers
714	7/21	1	1	23.	Yakety Yak	The Coasters
	1/6	4	2	24.	Great Balls Of Fire	Jerry Lee Lewis
	3/10	3	2	25.	26 Miles (Santa Catalina)	The Four Preps
	1/13	3	2	26.	Stood Up	Ricky Nelson
	3/17	3	2	27.	Sweet Little Sixteen	Chuck Berry
	10/13	2	2	28.	Rock-in Robin	Bobby Day
	3/31	2	2	29.	Lollipop	The Chordettes
	1/6	1	2	30.	All The Way	Frank Sinatra
	4/28	1	2	31.	Wear My Ring Around Your Neck	Elvis Presley
	12/15	1	2	32.	Problems	The Everly Brothers
	6/16	3	3	33.	Secretly	Jimmie Rodgers
	10/20	3	3	34.	Topsy II	Cozy Cole
	6/9	2	3	35.	Big Man	The Four Preps
	2/10	2	3	36.	Short Shorts	Royal Teens
	8/18	1	3	37.	My True Love	Jack Scott
	8/4	1	3	38.	Splish Splash	Bobby Darin
	3/24	1	3	39.	Are You Sincere	Andy Williams
	3/10	5	4	40.	A Wonderful Time Up There	Pat Boone

TOP 40 HITS   1959

RANK	PEAK DATE	PEAK WKS	PEAK POS	TITLE	ARTIST
27	10/5	9	1	1. Mack The Knife	Bobby Darin
91	6/1	6	1	2. The Battle Of New Orleans	Johnny Horton
136	3/9	5	1	3. Venus	Frankie Avalon
200	2/9	4	1	4. Stagger Lee	Lloyd Price
203	8/24	4	1	5. The Three Bells	The Browns
204	7/13	4	1	6. Lonely Boy	Paul Anka
237	4/13	4	1	7. Come Softly To Me	Fleetwoods
287	1/19	3	1	8. Smoke Gets In Your Eyes	The Platters
429	12/14	2	1	9. Heartaches By The Number	Guy Mitchell
461	9/21	2	1	10. Sleep Walk	Santo & Johnny
516	5/18	2	1	11. Kansas City	Wilbert Harrison
572	8/10	2	1	12. A Big Hunk O' Love	Elvis Presley
666	11/16	1	1	13. Mr. Blue	The Fleetwoods
724	12/28	1	1	14. Why	Frankie Avalon
810	5/11	1	1	15. The Happy Organ	Dave 'Baby' Cortez
	10/5	3	2	16. Put Your Head On My Shoulder	Paul Anka
	6/15	3	2	17. Personality	Lloyd Price
	3/9	3	2	18. Charlie Brown	The Coasters
	2/23	2	2	19. Donna	Ritchie Valens
	2/9	2	2	20. 16 Candles	The Crests
	1/19	2	2	21. My Happiness	Connie Francis
	5/11	2	2	22. Sorry (I Ran All the Way Home)	The Impalas
	8/24	2	2	23. Sea Of Love	Phil Phillips
	6/8	1	2	24. Dream Lover	Bobby Darin
	11/30	1	2	25. Don't You Know	Della Reese
	8/17	1	2	26. There Goes My Baby	The Drifters
	2/2	1	2	27. The All American Boy	Bill Parsons
	4/27	1	2	28. (Now and Then There's) A Fool Such As I	Elvis Presley
	8/3	3	3	29. My Heart Is An Open Book	Carl Dobkins, Jr.
	4/13	2	3	30. Pink Shoe Laces	Dodie Stevens
	12/28	2	3	31. The Big Hurt	Miss Toni Fisher
	9/14	2	3	32. I'm Gonna Get Married	Lloyd Price
	7/20	2	3	33. Tiger	Fabian
	3/16	2	3	34. Alvin's Harmonica	The Chipmunks
	4/6	1	3	35. It's Just A Matter Of Time	Brook Benton
	8/24	1	3	36. Lavender-Blue	Sammy Turner
	9/21	3	4	37. ('Til) I Kissed You	The Everly Brothers
	7/13	3	4	38. Waterloo	Stonewall Jackson
	10/19	2	4	39. Teen Beat	Sandy Nelson
	6/1	2	4	40. Quiet Village	Martin Denny

RANK	PEAK DATE	PEAK WKS	PEAK POS	TITLE	ARTIST
34	2/22	9	1	1. The Theme From "A Summer Place"	Percy Faith
101	11/28	6	1	2. Are You Lonesome To-night?	Elvis Presley
125	8/15	5	1	3. It's Now Or Never	Elvis Presley
145	5/23	5	1	4. Cathy's Clown	The Everly Brothers
206	4/25	4	1	5. Stuck On You	Elvis Presley
272	7/18	3	1	6. I'm Sorry	Brenda Lee
290	1/18	3	1	7. Running Bear	Johnny Preston
301	10/17	3	1	8. Save The Last Dance For Me	The Drifters
433	2/8	2	1	9. Teen Angel	Mark Dinning
434	9/26	2	1	10. My Heart Has A Mind Of Its Own	Connie Francis
451	1/4	2	1	11. El Paso	Marty Robbins
491	6/27	2	1	12. Everybody's Somebody's Fool	Connie Francis
246	9/19	1	1	13. The Twist	Chubby Checker
				re-entered at #1 in 1962	
766	8/8	1	1	14. Itsy Bitsy Teenie Weenie Yellow Polkadot Bikini	Brian Hyland
768	7/11	1	1	15. Alley-Oop	Hollywood Argyles
857	10/10	1	1	16. Mr. Custer	Larry Verne
908	10/24	1	1	17. I Want To Be Wanted	Brenda Lee
944	11/21	1	1	18. Stay	Maurice Williams & Zodiacs
960	11/14	1	1	19. Georgia On My Mind	Ray Charles
	11/28	4	2	20. Last Date	Floyd Cramer
	4/18	4	2	21. Greenfields	The Brothers Four
	3/7	3	2	22. He'll Have To Go	Jim Reeves
	10/3	2	2	23. Chain Gang	Sam Cooke
	4/4	2	2	24. Puppy Love	Paul Anka
	2/29	1	2	25. Handy Man	Jimmy Jones
	8/29	1	2	26. Walk—Don't Run	The Ventures
	7/25	1	2	27. Only The Lonely (Know How I Feel)	Roy Orbison
	3/28	1	2	28. Wild One	Bobby Rydell
	11/14	1	2	29. Poetry In Motion	Johnny Tillotson
	5/23	3	3	30. Good Timin'	Jimmy Jones
	6/13	2	3	31. Burning Bridges	Jack Scott
	12/12	1	3	32. A Thousand Stars	Kathy Young with The Innocents
	5/2	1	3	33. Sixteen Reasons	Connie Stevens
	4/25	1	3	34. Sink The Bismarck	Johnny Horton
	1/11	1	3	35. Way Down Yonder In New Orleans	Freddie Cannon
	2/8	1	3	36. Where Or When	Dion & The Belmonts
	11/14	1	3	37. You Talk Too Much	Joe Jones
	5/9	2	4	38. Night	Jackie Wilson
	5/30	2	4	39. He'll Have To Stay	Jeanne Black
	7/4	2	4	40. Because They're Young	Duane Eddy & The Rebels

RANK	PEAK DATE	PEAK WKS	PEAK POS		TITLE	ARTIST
62	7/10	7	1	1.	Tossin' And Turnin'	Bobby Lewis
140	11/6	5	1	2.	Big Bad John	Jimmy Dean
221	4/24	4	1	3.	Runaway	Del Shannon
289	1/9	3	1	4.	Wonderland By Night	Bert Kaempfert
322	2/27	3	1	5.	Pony Time	Chubby Checker
332	12/18	3	1	6.	The Lion Sleeps Tonight	The Tokens
340	4/3	3	1	7.	Blue Moon	The Marcels
368	9/18	3	1	8.	Take Good Care Of My Baby	Bobby Vee
462	2/13	2	1	9.	Calcutta	Lawrence Welk
475	10/23	2	1	10.	Runaround Sue	Dion
480	9/4	2	1	11.	Michael	The Highwaymen
498	5/29	2	1	12.	Travelin' Man	Ricky Nelson
518	6/26	2	1	13.	Quarter To Three	U.S. Bonds
522	10/9	2	1	14.	Hit The Road Jack	Ray Charles
524	3/20	2	1	15.	Surrender	Elvis Presley
536	1/30	2	1	16.	Will You Love Me Tomorrow	The Shirelles
769	5/22	1	1	17.	Mother-In-Law	Ernie K-Doe
784	12/11	1	1	18.	Please Mr. Postman	The Marvelettes
837	8/28	1	1	19.	Wooden Heart	Joe Dowell
924	6/19	1	1	20.	Moody River	Pat Boone
966	6/5	1	1	21.	Running Scared	Roy Orbison
	7/10	3	2	22.	The Boll Weevil Song	Brook Benton
	7/31	3	2	23.	I Like It Like That, Part 1	Chris Kenner
	10/23	2	2	24.	Bristol Stomp	The Dovells
	4/3	2	2	25.	Apache	Jorgen Ingmann
	9/25	2	2	26.	The Mountain's High	Dick & DeeDee
	1/23	1	2	27.	Exodus	Ferrante & Teicher
	6/26	1	2	28.	Raindrops	Dee Clark
	2/20	1	2	29.	Shop Around	The Miracles
	12/25	1	2	30.	Run To Him	Bobby Vee
	10/9	1	2	31.	Crying	Roy Orbison
	5/29	1	2	32.	Daddy's Home	Shep & The Limelites
	3/27	2	3	33.	Dedicated To The One I Love	The Shirelles
	5/8	2	3	34.	A Hundred Pounds Of Clay	Gene McDaniels
	12/4	2	3	35.	Goodbye Cruel World	James Darren
	3/6	2	3	36.	Wheels	The String-A-Longs
	8/7	2	3	37.	Last Night	Mar-Keys
	11/13	2	3	38.	Fool #1	Brenda Lee
	9/11	2	3	39.	My True Story	The Jive Five
	3/20	1	3	40.	Don't Worry	Marty Robbins

RANK	PEAK DATE	PEAK WKS	PEAK POS	TITLE	ARTIST
130	6/2	5	1	1. I Can't Stop Loving You	Ray Charles
137	11/17	5	1	2. Big Girls Don't Cry	The 4 Seasons
151	9/15	5	1	3. Sherry	The 4 Seasons
207	7/14	4	1	4. Roses Are Red (My Love)	Bobby Vinton
278	1/27	3	1	5. Peppermint Twist - Part I	Joey Dee & the Starliters
330	12/22	3	1	6. Telstar	The Tornadoes
333	5/5	3	1	7. Soldier Boy	The Shirelles
336	3/10	3	1	8. Hey! Baby	Bruce Channel
338	2/17	3	1	9. Duke Of Earl	Gene Chandler
246	1/13	2	1	10. The Twist	Chubby Checker
				re-entry of 1960 #1 hit	
468	4/7	2	1	11. Johnny Angel	Shelley Fabares
555	11/3	2	1	12. He's A Rebel	The Crystals
560	8/11	2	1	13. Breaking Up Is Hard To Do	Neil Sedaka
561	10/20	2	1	14. Monster Mash	Bobby "Boris" Pickett
566	4/21	2	1	15. Good Luck Charm	Elvis Presley
617	9/1	2	1	16. Sheila	Tommy Roe
669	5/26	1	1	17. Stranger On The Shore	Mr. Acker Bilk
721	7/7	1	1	18. The Stripper	David Rose
836	8/25	1	1	19. The Loco-Motion	Little Eva
936	3/31	1	1	20. Don't Break The Heart That Loves You	Connie Francis
	11/17	5	2	21. Return To Sender	Elvis Presley
	12/22	2	2	22. Limbo Rock	Chubby Checker
	5/5	2	2	23. Mashed Potato Time	Dee Dee Sharp
	9/22	2	2	24. Ramblin' Rose	Nat King Cole
	7/21	2	2	25. The Wah Watusi	The Orlons
	2/3	1	2	26. Can't Help Falling In Love	Elvis Presley
	2/24	1	2	27. The Wanderer	Dion
	3/17	1	2	28. Midnight In Moscow	Kenny Ball
	9/8	1	2	29. You Don't Know Me	Ray Charles
	11/3	1	2	30. Only Love Can Break A Heart	Gene Pitney
	12/1	4	3	31. Bobby's Girl	Marcie Blane
	10/20	3	3	32. Do You Love Me	The Contours
	11/10	2	3	33. All Alone Am I	Brenda Lee
	6/23	2	3	34. Palisades Park	Freddy Cannon
	7/28	2	3	35. Sealed With A Kiss	Brian Hyland
	4/14	1	3	36. Slow Twistin'	Chubby Checker (with Dee Dee Sharp)
	2/24	1	3	37. Norman	Sue Thompson
	9/29	1	3	38. Green Onions	Booker T. & The MG's
	6/16	1	3	39. It Keeps Right On A-Hurtin'	Johnny Tillotson
	1/27	1	3	40. I Know (You Don't Love Me No More)	Barbara George

TOP 40 HITS   1963

RANK	PEAK DATE	PEAK WKS	PEAK POS		TITLE	ARTIST
141	10/12	5	1	1.	Sugar Shack	Jimmy Gilmer & The Fireballs
222	3/30	4	1	2.	He's So Fine	The Chiffons
225	12/7	4	1	3.	Dominique	The Singing Nun
310	2/9	3	1	4.	Hey Paula	Paul & Paula
311	8/31	3	1	5.	My Boyfriend's Back	The Angels
335	9/21	3	1	6.	Blue Velvet	Bobby Vinton
337	6/15	3	1	7.	Sukiyaki	Kyu Sakamoto
341	4/27	3	1	8.	I Will Follow Him	Little Peggy March
365	8/10	3	1	9.	Fingertips - Pt 2	Little Stevie Wonder
367	3/2	3	1	10.	Walk Like A Man	The 4 Seasons
474	1/12	2	1	11.	Go Away Little Girl	Steve Lawrence
559	11/23	2	1	12.	I'm Leaving It Up To You	Dale & Grace
567	7/20	2	1	13.	Surf City	Jan & Dean
568	6/1	2	1	14.	It's My Party	Lesley Gore
569	1/26	2	1	15.	Walk Right In	The Rooftop Singers
573	7/6	2	1	16.	Easier Said Than Done	The Essex
618	5/18	2	1	17.	If You Wanna Be Happy	Jimmy Soul
841	8/3	1	1	18.	So Much In Love	The Tymes
842	11/16	1	1	19.	Deep Purple	Nino Tempo & April Stevens
935	3/23	1	1	20.	Our Day Will Come	Ruby & The Romantics
997	12/14	6	2	21.	Louie Louie	The Kingsmen
	4/13	4	2	22.	Can't Get Used To Losing You	Andy Williams
	2/23	3	2	23.	Ruby Baby	Dion
	10/12	3	2	24.	Be My Baby	The Ronettes
	8/24	3	2	25.	Hello Mudduh, Hello Fadduh!	Allan Sherman
	9/28	2	2	26.	Sally, Go 'Round The Roses	The Jaynetts
	8/17	1	2	27.	Blowin' In The Wind	Peter, Paul & Mary
	11/23	1	2	28.	Washington Square	The Village Stompers
	8/10	1	2	29.	Wipe Out	The Surfaris
	3/23	1	2	30.	The End Of The World	Skeeter Davis
	5/11	1	2	31.	Puff (The Magic Dragon)	Peter, Paul & Mary
	9/7	3	3	32.	If I Had A Hammer	Trini Lopez
	3/16	2	3	33.	You're The Reason I'm Living	Bobby Darin
	2/2	2	3	34.	The Night Has A Thousand Eyes	Bobby Vee
	12/7	2	3	35.	Everybody	Tommy Roe
	8/10	2	3	36.	(You're the) Devil In Disguise	Elvis Presley
	6/22	2	3	37.	Hello Stranger	Barbara Lewis
	3/9	1	3	38.	Rhythm Of The Rain	The Cascades
	5/25	1	3	39.	Surfin' U.S.A.	Beach Boys
	6/1	1	3	40.	I Love You Because	Al Martino

TOP 40 HITS   1964

RANK	PEAK DATE	PEAK WKS	PEAK POS	#	TITLE	ARTIST
65	2/1	7	1	1.	I Want To Hold Your Hand	The Beatles
152	4/4	5	1	2.	Can't Buy Me Love	The Beatles
226	1/4	4	1	3.	There! I've Said It Again	Bobby Vinton
239	10/31	4	1	4.	Baby Love	The Supremes
324	9/26	3	1	5.	Oh, Pretty Woman	Roy Orbison
345	9/5	3	1	6.	The House Of The Rising Sun	The Animals
370	6/6	3	1	7.	Chapel Of Love	The Dixie Cups
373	12/26	3	1	8.	I Feel Fine	The Beatles
422	3/21	2	1	9.	She Loves You	The Beatles
465	7/4	2	1	10.	I Get Around	The Beach Boys
472	12/19	2	1	11.	Come See About Me	The Supremes
473	8/22	2	1	12.	Where Did Our Love Go	The Supremes
479	10/17	2	1	13.	Do Wah Diddy Diddy	Manfred Mann
511	5/16	2	1	14.	My Guy	Mary Wells
520	8/1	2	1	15.	A Hard Day's Night	The Beatles
570	7/18	2	1	16.	Rag Doll	The 4 Seasons
653	5/9	1	1	17.	Hello, Dolly!	Louis Armstrong
720	12/12	1	1	18.	Mr. Lonely	Bobby Vinton
765	8/15	1	1	19.	Everybody Loves Somebody	Dean Martin
773	6/27	1	1	20.	A World Without Love	Peter & Gordon
860	12/5	1	1	21.	Ringo	Lorne Greene
930	5/30	1	1	22.	Love Me Do	The Beatles
961	11/28	1	1	23.	Leader Of The Pack	The Shangri-Las
	4/4	4	2	24.	Twist And Shout	The Beatles
	2/1	3	2	25.	You Don't Own Me	Lesley Gore
	10/17	2	2	26.	Dancing In The Street	Martha & The Vandellas
	9/19	2	2	27.	Bread And Butter	The Newbeats
	7/11	2	2	28.	Memphis	Johnny Rivers
	11/7	1	2	29.	Last Kiss	J. Frank Wilson & The Cavaliers
	12/12	1	2	30.	She's Not There	The Zombies
	7/4	1	2	31.	My Boy Lollipop	Millie Small
	5/9	1	2	32.	Do You Want To Know A Secret	The Beatles
	2/22	3	3	33.	Dawn (Go Away)	The Four Seasons
	4/11	2	3	34.	Suspicion	Terry Stafford
	3/14	2	3	35.	Please Please Me	The Beatles
	1/11	2	3	36.	Popsicles And Icicles	The Murmaids
	2/1	2	3	37.	Out Of Limits	The Marketts
	11/21	2	3	38.	Come A Little Bit Closer	Jay & The Americans
	6/13	1	3	39.	Love Me With All Your Heart (Cuando Calienta El Sol)	Ray Charles Singers
	8/1	1	3	40.	The Little Old Lady (From Pasadena)	Jan & Dean

RANK	PEAK DATE	PEAK WKS	PEAK POS		TITLE	ARTIST
223	7/10	4	1	1.	(I Can't Get No) Satisfaction	The Rolling Stones
245	10/9	4	1	2.	Yesterday	The Beatles
339	12/4	3	1	3.	Turn! Turn! Turn! (To Everything There Is A Season)	The Byrds
372	5/1	3	1	4.	Mrs. Brown You've Got A Lovely Daughter	Herman's Hermits
374	8/14	3	1	5.	I Got You Babe	Sonny & Cher
381	9/4	3	1	6.	Help!	The Beatles
437	6/19	2	1	7.	I Can't Help Myself	Four Tops
463	2/6	2	1	8.	You've Lost That Lovin' Feelin'	The Righteous Brothers
467	1/23	2	1	9.	Downtown	Petula Clark
481	2/20	2	1	10.	This Diamond Ring	Gary Lewis & The Playboys
525	3/27	2	1	11.	Stop! In The Name Of Love	The Supremes
565	5/29	2	1	12.	Help Me, Rhonda	The Beach Boys
619	11/6	2	1	13.	Get Off Of My Cloud	The Rolling Stones
625	11/20	2	1	14.	I Hear A Symphony	The Supremes
627	4/10	2	1	15.	I'm Telling You Now	Freddie & The Dreamers
633	3/13	2	1	16.	Eight Days A Week	The Beatles
772	3/6	1	1	17.	My Girl	The Temptations
856	10/2	1	1	18.	Hang On Sloopy	The McCoys
859	6/26	1	1	19.	Mr. Tambourine Man	The Byrds
862	9/25	1	1	20.	Eve Of Destruction	Barry McGuire
932	12/25	1	1	21.	Over And Over	The Dave Clark Five
938	5/22	1	1	22.	Ticket To Ride	The Beatles
939	8/7	1	1	23.	I'm Henry VIII, I Am	Herman's Hermits
962	4/24	1	1	24.	Game Of Love	Wayne Fontana/Mindbenders
963	6/12	1	1	25.	Back In My Arms Again	The Supremes
	10/30	3	2	26.	A Lover's Concerto	The Toys
	6/5	2	2	27.	Wooly Bully	Sam The Sham & the Pharaohs
	3/27	2	2	28.	Can't You Hear My Heartbeat	Herman's Hermits
	9/4	2	2	29.	Like A Rolling Stone	Bob Dylan
	10/16	2	2	30.	Treat Her Right	Roy Head & The Traits
	5/8	2	2	31.	Count Me In	Gary Lewis & The Playboys
	11/20	1	2	32.	1-2-3	Len Barry
	8/21	1	2	33.	Save Your Heart For Me	Gary Lewis & The Playboys
	12/18	3	3	34.	I Got You (I Feel Good)	James Brown
	3/20	2	3	35.	The Birds And The Bees	Jewel Akens
	1/16	2	3	36.	Love Potion Number Nine	The Searchers
	1/30	2	3	37.	The Name Game	Shirley Ellis
	7/31	2	3	38.	What's New Pussycat?	Tom Jones
	8/28	2	3	39.	California Girls	The Beach Boys
	12/11	1	3	40.	Let's Hang On!	The 4 Seasons

RANK	PEAK DATE	PEAK WKS	PEAK POS		TITLE	ARTIST
66	12/31	7	1	1.	I'm A Believer	The Monkees
150	3/5	5	1	2.	The Ballad Of The Green Berets	SSgt Barry Sadler
294	12/3	3	1	3.	Winchester Cathedral	New Vaudeville Band
342	4/9	3	1	4.	(You're My) Soul And Inspiration	The Righteous Brothers
343	5/7	3	1	5.	Monday, Monday	The Mamas & The Papas
371	1/8	3	1	6.	We Can Work It Out	The Beatles
375	8/13	3	1	7.	Summer In The City	The Lovin' Spoonful
380	9/24	3	1	8.	Cherish	The Association
523	9/10	2	1	9.	You Can't Hurry Love	The Supremes
526	7/30	2	1	10.	Wild Thing	The Troggs
558	10/15	2	1	11.	Reach Out I'll Be There	Four Tops
576	6/11	2	1	12.	Paint It, Black	The Rolling Stones
621	5/28	2	1	13.	When A Man Loves A Woman	Percy Sledge
622	11/19	2	1	14.	You Keep Me Hangin' On	The Supremes
623	7/16	2	1	15.	Hanky Panky	Tommy James & The Shondells
626	2/5	2	1	16.	My Love	Petula Clark
628	1/1	2	1	17.	The Sounds Of Silence	Simon & Garfunkel
632	6/25	2	1	18.	Paperback Writer	The Beatles
725	10/29	1	1	19.	96 Tears	? & The Mysterians
726	11/5	1	1	20.	Last Train To Clarksville	The Monkees
840	11/12	1	1	21.	Poor Side Of Town	Johnny Rivers
843	2/26	1	1	22.	These Boots Are Made For Walkin'	Nancy Sinatra
844	12/10	1	1	23.	Good Vibrations	The Beach Boys
845	4/30	1	1	24.	Good Lovin'	The Young Rascals
852	7/2	1	1	25.	Strangers In The Night	Frank Sinatra
858	9/3	1	1	26.	Sunshine Superman	Donovan
933	2/19	1	1	27.	Lightnin' Strikes	Lou Christie
	12/31	4	2	28.	Snoopy Vs. The Red Baron	The Royal Guardsmen
	12/10	3	2	29.	Mellow Yellow	Donovan
	3/19	3	2	30.	19th Nervous Breakdown	The Rolling Stones
	8/6	2	2	31.	Lil' Red Riding Hood	Sam The Sham & The Pharaohs
	4/9	2	2	32.	Daydream	The Lovin' Spoonful
	8/20	2	2	33.	Sunny	Bobby Hebb
	6/11	2	2	34.	Did You Ever Have To Make Up Your Mind?	The Lovin' Spoonful
	5/28	2	2	35.	A Groovy Kind Of Love	The Mindbenders
	1/29	2	2	36.	Barbara Ann	The Beach Boys
	7/9	1	2	37.	Red Rubber Ball	The Cyrkle
	4/23	1	2	38.	Bang Bang (My Baby Shot Me Down)	Cher
	9/17	1	2	39.	Yellow Submarine	The Beatles
	5/21	1	2	40.	Rainy Day Women #12 & 35	Bob Dylan

TOP 40 HITS 1967

RANK	PEAK DATE	PEAK WKS	PEAK POS	TITLE	ARTIST
144	10/21	5	1	1. To Sir With Love	Lulu
209	12/2	4	1	2. Daydream Believer	The Monkees
220	7/1	4	1	3. Windy	The Association
224	8/26	4	1	4. Ode To Billie Joe	Bobbie Gentry
227	4/15	4	1	5. Somethin' Stupid	Nancy Sinatra & Frank Sinatra
228	5/20	4	1	6. Groovin'	The Young Rascals
235	9/23	4	1	7. The Letter	The Box Tops
303	7/29	3	1	8. Light My Fire	The Doors
309	3/25	3	1	9. Happy Together	The Turtles
344	12/30	3	1	10. Hello Goodbye	The Beatles
571	6/3	2	1	11. Respect	Aretha Franklin
574	2/18	2	1	12. Kind Of A Drag	The Buckinghams
719	11/25	1	1	13. Incense And Peppermints	Strawberry Alarm Clock
861	3/11	1	1	14. Love Is Here And Now You're Gone	The Supremes
863	3/4	1	1	15. Ruby Tuesday	The Rolling Stones
864	8/19	1	1	16. All You Need Is Love	The Beatles
937	5/13	1	1	17. The Happening	The Supremes
965	3/18	1	1	18. Penny Lane	The Beatles
	12/16	3	2	19. I Heard It Through The Grapevine	Gladys Knight & The Pips
	11/4	3	2	20. Soul Man	Sam & Dave
	3/25	3	2	21. Dedicated To The One I Love	The Mamas & The Papas
	7/8	2	2	22. Little Bit O'Soul	The Music Explosion
	12/2	2	2	23. The Rain, The Park & Other Things	The Cowsills
	2/4	2	2	24. Georgy Girl	The Seekers
	10/7	2	2	25. Never My Love	The Association
	7/29	2	2	26. I Was Made To Love Her	Stevie Wonder
	9/9	2	2	27. Reflections	Diana Ross & The Supremes
	7/22	1	2	28. Can't Take My Eyes Off You	Frankie Valli
	1/28	1	2	29. Tell It Like It Is	Aaron Neville
	5/13	1	2	30. Sweet Soul Music	Arthur Conley
	4/29	1	2	31. A Little Bit Me, A Little Bit You	The Monkees
	9/9	3	3	32. Come Back When You Grow Up	Bobby Vee & The Strangers
	5/27	3	3	33. I Got Rhythm	The Happenings
	11/4	2	3	34. It Must Be Him	Vikki Carr
	8/19	2	3	35. Pleasant Valley Sunday	The Monkees
	3/11	2	3	36. Baby I Need Your Lovin'	Johnny Rivers
	6/17	2	3	37. She'd Rather Be With Me	The Turtles
	4/15	1	3	38. This Is My Song	Petula Clark
	5/27	4	4	39. Release Me (And Let Me Love Again)	Engelbert Humperdinck
	7/1	4	4	40. San Francisco (Be Sure To Wear Flowers In Your Hair)	Scott McKenzie

TOP 40 HITS   1968

RANK	PEAK DATE	PEAK WKS	PEAK POS		TITLE	ARTIST
32	9/28	9	1	1.	Hey Jude	The Beatles
68	12/14	7	1	2.	I Heard It Through The Grapevine	Marvin Gaye
134	2/10	5	1	3.	Love Is Blue	Paul Mauriat
142	4/13	5	1	4.	Honey	Bobby Goldsboro
147	8/17	5	1	5.	People Got To Be Free	The Rascals
192	3/16	4	1	6.	(Sittin' On) The Dock Of The Bay	Otis Redding
238	6/22	4	1	7.	This Guy's In Love With You	Herb Alpert
366	6/1	3	1	8.	Mrs. Robinson	Simon & Garfunkel
418	11/30	2	1	9.	Love Child	Diana Ross & The Supremes
470	5/18	2	1	10.	Tighten Up	Archie Bell & The Drells
482	8/3	2	1	11.	Hello, I Love You	The Doors
509	1/20	2	1	12.	Judy In Disguise (With Glasses)	John Fred & His Playboy Band
575	7/20	2	1	13.	Grazing In The Grass	Hugh Masekela
727	9/21	1	1	14.	Harper Valley P.T.A.	Jeannie C. Riley
847	2/3	1	1	15.	Green Tambourine	The Lemon Pipers
	2/24	4	2	16.	(Theme From) Valley Of The Dolls	Dionne Warwick
	4/6	3	2	17.	Young Girl	Union Gap feat. Gary Puckett
	11/2	3	2	18.	Those Were The Days	Mary Hopkin
	6/29	3	2	19.	The Horse	Cliff Nobles & Co.
	8/24	3	2	20.	Born To Be Wild	Steppenwolf
	12/28	2	2	21.	For Once In My Life	Stevie Wonder
	1/20	2	2	22.	Chain Of Fools	Aretha Franklin
	4/27	2	2	23.	Cry Like A Baby	The Box Tops
	8/3	2	2	24.	Classical Gas	Mason Williams
	7/20	2	2	25.	Lady Willpower	Gary Puckett & The Union Gap
	10/26	1	2	26.	Little Green Apples	O.C. Smith
	6/1	1	2	27.	The Good, The Bad And The Ugly	Hugo Montenegro
	10/19	1	2	28.	Fire	Crazy World Of Arthur Brown
	6/22	1	2	29.	MacArthur Park	Richard Harris
	7/27	3	3	30.	Stoned Soul Picnic	The 5th Dimension
	2/10	3	3	31.	Spooky	Classics IV
	7/6	3	3	32.	Jumpin' Jack Flash	The Rolling Stones
	8/31	3	3	33.	Light My Fire	Jose Feliciano
	5/25	2	3	34.	A Beautiful Morning	The Rascals
	3/30	2	3	35.	Valleri	The Monkees
	11/30	1	3	36.	Magic Carpet Ride	Steppenwolf
	6/15	1	3	37.	Mony Mony	Tommy James & The Shondells
	3/9	4	4	38.	Simon Says	1910 Fruitgum Co.
	1/13	3	4	39.	Woman, Woman	Union Gap feat. Gary Puckett
	2/17	3	4	40.	I Wish It Would Rain	The Temptations

135

RANK	PEAK DATE	PEAK WKS	PEAK POS	TITLE	ARTIST
97	4/12	6	1	1. Aquarius/Let The Sunshine In	The 5th Dimension
106	7/12	6	1	2. In The Year 2525 (Exordium & Terminus)	Zager & Evans
149	5/24	5	1	3. Get Back	The Beatles with Billy Preston
184	9/20	4	1	4. Sugar, Sugar	The Archies
193	8/23	4	1	5. Honky Tonk Women	The Rolling Stones
216	2/15	4	1	6. Everyday People	Sly & The Family Stone
219	3/15	4	1	7. Dizzy	Tommy Roe
326	11/8	3	1	8. Wedding Bell Blues	The 5th Dimension
417	10/18	2	1	9. I Can't Get Next To You	The Temptations
419	2/1	2	1	10. Crimson And Clover	Tommy James & The Shondells
508	12/6	2	1	11. Na Na Hey Hey Kiss Him Goodbye	Steam
519	6/28	2	1	12. Love Theme From Romeo & Juliet	Henry Mancini
681	12/20	1	1	13. Leaving On A Jet Plane	Peter, Paul & Mary
708	11/29	1	1	14. Come Together	The Beatles
712	12/27	1	1	15. Someday We'll Be Together	Diana Ross & The Supremes
909	11/1	1	1	16. Suspicious Minds	Elvis Presley
	7/26	3	2	17. Crystal Blue Persuasion	Tommy James & The Shondells
	3/8	3	2	18. Proud Mary	Creedence Clearwater Revival
	7/5	3	2	19. Spinning Wheel	Blood, Sweat & Tears
	8/23	3	2	20. A Boy Named Sue	Johnny Cash
	4/12	3	2	21. You've Made Me So Very Happy	Blood, Sweat & Tears
	5/10	2	2	22. Hair	The Cowsills
	1/11	2	2	23. I'm Gonna Make You Love Me	Supremes & Temptations
	10/18	2	2	24. Hot Fun In The Summertime	Sly & The Family Stone
	10/4	2	2	25. Jean	Oliver
	5/31	2	2	26. Love (Can Make You Happy)	Mercy
	9/27	1	2	27. Green River	Creedence Clearwater Revival
	11/22	1	2	28. Take A Letter Maria	R.B. Greaves
	5/3	1	2	29. It's Your Thing	The Isley Brothers
	11/29	1	2	30. And When I Die	Blood, Sweat & Tears
	6/28	1	2	31. Bad Moon Rising	Creedence Clearwater Revival
	3/29	1	2	32. Traces	Classics IV Feat. Dennis Yost
	2/22	3	3	33. Build Me Up Buttercup	The Foundations
	10/4	2	3	34. Little Woman	Bobby Sherman
	2/1	2	3	35. Worst That Could Happen	Brooklyn Bridge
	3/29	2	3	36. Time Of The Season	The Zombies
	7/12	2	3	37. Good Morning Starshine	Oliver
	11/15	2	3	38. Something	The Beatles
	1/11	1	3	39. Wichita Lineman	Glen Campbell
	12/20	1	3	40. Down On The Corner	Creedence Clearwater Revival

TOP 40 HITS   1970

RANK	PEAK DATE	PEAK WKS	PEAK POS		TITLE	ARTIST
104	2/28	6	1	1.	Bridge Over Troubled Water	Simon & Garfunkel
127	10/17	5	1	2.	I'll Be There	The Jackson 5
174	1/3	4	1	3.	Raindrops Keep Fallin' On My Head	B.J. Thomas
191	7/25	4	1	4.	(They Long To Be) Close To You	Carpenters
208	12/26	4	1	5.	My Sweet Lord	George Harrison
276	11/21	3	1	6.	I Think I Love You	The Partridge Family
308	9/19	3	1	7.	Ain't No Mountain High Enough	Diana Ross
325	5/9	3	1	8.	American Woman	The Guess Who
331	8/29	3	1	9.	War	Edwin Starr
423	4/11	2	1	10.	Let It Be	The Beatles
435	12/12	2	1	11.	The Tears Of A Clown	Smokey Robinson & The Miracles
469	7/11	2	1	12.	Mama Told Me (Not To Come)	Three Dog Night
476	4/25	2	1	13.	ABC	The Jackson 5
477	6/27	2	1	14.	The Love You Save	The Jackson 5
562	2/14	2	1	15.	Thank You (Falettinme Be Mice Elf Agin)	Sly & The Family Stone
606	5/30	2	1	16.	Everything Is Beautiful	Ray Stevens
624	6/13	2	1	17.	The Long And Winding Road	The Beatles
687	8/22	1	1	18.	Make It With You	Bread
706	1/31	1	1	19.	I Want You Back	The Jackson 5
723	2/7	1	1	20.	Venus	The Shocking Blue
812	10/10	1	1	21.	Cracklin' Rosie	Neil Diamond
	10/31	4	2	22.	We've Only Just Begun	Carpenters
	12/26	2	2	23.	One Less Bell To Answer	The 5th Dimension
	6/6	2	2	24.	Which Way You Goin' Billy?	The Poppy Family
	3/7	2	2	25.	Travelin' Band	Creedence Clearwater Revival
	10/3	1	2	26.	Lookin' Out My Back Door	Creedence Clearwater Revival
	2/21	1	2	27.	Hey There Lonely Girl	Eddie Holman
	3/21	1	2	28.	The Rapper	The Jaggerz
	5/23	1	2	29.	Vehicle	The Ides Of March
	6/27	3	3	30.	Ball Of Confusion (That's What The World Is Today)	The Temptations
	10/31	3	3	31.	Fire And Rain	James Taylor
	4/18	3	3	32.	Spirit In The Sky	Norman Greenbaum
	3/28	3	3	33.	Instant Karma (We All Shine On)	John Ono Lennon
	12/5	2	3	34.	Gypsy Woman	Brian Hyland
	10/3	2	3	35.	Candida	Dawn
	10/17	2	3	36.	Green-Eyed Lady	Sugarloaf
	8/8	2	3	37.	Signed, Sealed, Delivered I'm Yours	Stevie Wonder
	5/30	2	3	38.	Love On A Two-Way Street	The Moments
	7/25	1	3	39.	Band Of Gold	Freda Payne
	8/22	1	3	40.	Spill The Wine	Eric Burdon & War

RANK	PEAK DATE	PEAK WKS	PEAK POS		TITLE	ARTIST
100	4/17	6	1	1.	Joy To The World	Three Dog Night
129	10/2	5	1	2.	Maggie May	Rod Stewart
135	6/19	5	1	3.	It's Too Late	Carole King
148	2/13	5	1	4.	One Bad Apple	The Osmonds
205	8/7	4	1	5.	How Can You Mend A Broken Heart	The Bee Gees
277	1/23	3	1	6.	Knock Three Times	Dawn
293	12/25	3	1	7.	Brand New Key	Melanie
306	9/11	3	1	8.	Go Away Little Girl	Donny Osmond
307	12/4	3	1	9.	Family Affair	Sly & The Family Stone
458	11/6	2	1	10.	Gypsys, Tramps & Thieves	Cher
466	4/3	2	1	11.	Just My Imagination (Running Away With Me)	The Temptations
478	11/20	2	1	12.	Theme From Shaft	Isaac Hayes
517	3/20	2	1	13.	Me And Bobby McGee	Janis Joplin
521	5/29	2	1	14.	Brown Sugar	The Rolling Stones
710	7/24	1	1	15.	Indian Reservation (The Lament Of The Cherokee Reservation Indian)	Raiders
764	6/12	1	1	16.	Want Ads	The Honey Cone
770	7/31	1	1	17.	You've Got A Friend	James Taylor
846	9/4	1	1	18.	Uncle Albert/Admiral Halsey	Paul & Linda McCartney
	4/10	3	2	19.	What's Going On	Marvin Gaye
	5/8	3	2	20.	Never Can Say Goodbye	The Jackson 5
	8/14	2	2	21.	Mr. Big Stuff	Jean Knight
	10/16	2	2	22.	Superstar	Carpenters
	6/19	2	2	23.	Rainy Days And Mondays	Carpenters
	9/11	2	2	24.	Spanish Harlem	Aretha Franklin
	2/27	2	2	25.	Mama's Pearl	The Jackson 5
	8/28	1	2	26.	Take Me Home, Country Roads	John Denver
	3/20	1	2	27.	She's A Lady	Tom Jones
	5/1	1	2	28.	Put Your Hand In The Hand	Ocean
	10/16	3	3	29.	Yo-Yo	The Osmonds
	12/11	2	3	30.	Have You Seen Her	Chi-Lites
	7/3	2	3	31.	Treat Her Like A Lady	Cornelius Brothers & Sister Rose
	3/13	2	3	32.	For All We Know	Carpenters
	2/13	2	3	33.	Rose Garden	Lynn Anderson
	9/4	2	3	34.	Smiling Faces Sometimes	The Undisputed Truth
	9/18	2	3	35.	Ain't No Sunshine	Bill Withers
	11/13	2	3	36.	Imagine	John Lennon
	11/27	2	3	37.	Baby I'm-A Want You	Bread
	10/2	1	3	38.	The Night They Drove Old Dixie Down	Joan Baez
	1/30	1	3	39.	Lonely Days	Bee Gees
	8/28	1	3	40.	Signs	Five Man Electrical Band

TOP 40 HITS 1972

RANK	PEAK DATE	PEAK WKS	PEAK POS		TITLE	ARTIST
98	4/15	6	1	1.	The First Time Ever I Saw Your Face	Roberta Flack
99	7/29	6	1	2.	Alone Again (Naturally)	Gilbert O'Sullivan
190	1/15	4	1	3.	American Pie - Parts I & II	Don McLean
217	2/19	4	1	4.	Without You	Nilsson
232	11/4	4	1	5.	I Can See Clearly Now	Johnny Nash
295	3/25	3	1	6.	A Horse With No Name	America
305	9/23	3	1	7.	Baby Don't Get Hooked On Me	Mac Davis
323	12/16	3	1	8.	Me And Mrs. Jones	Billy Paul
349	6/10	3	1	9.	The Candy Man	Sammy Davis, Jr.
354	7/8	3	1	10.	Lean On Me	Bill Withers
614	10/21	2	1	11.	My Ding-A-Ling	Chuck Berry
685	8/26	1	1	12.	Brandy (You're A Fine Girl)	Looking Glass
713	2/12	1	1	13.	Let's Stay Together	Al Green
751	12/9	1	1	14.	I Am Woman	Helen Reddy
760	6/3	1	1	15.	I'll Take You There	The Staple Singers
767	3/18	1	1	16.	Heart Of Gold	Neil Young
813	5/27	1	1	17.	Oh Girl	Chi-Lites
849	10/14	1	1	18.	Ben	Michael Jackson
923	12/2	1	1	19.	Papa Was A Rollin' Stone	The Temptations
926	7/1	1	1	20.	Song Sung Blue	Neil Diamond
964	9/16	1	1	21.	Black & White	Three Dog Night
	5/6	2	2	22.	I Gotcha	Joe Tex
	9/2	2	2	23.	Long Cool Woman (In A Black Dress)	The Hollies
	7/15	2	2	24.	Too Late To Turn Back Now	Cornelius Brothers & Sister Rose
	4/22	2	2	25.	Rockin' Robin	Michael Jackson
	11/4	2	2	26.	Nights In White Satin	The Moody Blues
	12/30	2	2	27.	Clair	Gilbert O'Sullivan
	2/26	2	2	28.	Hurting Each Other	Carpenters
	11/18	2	2	29.	I'd Love You To Want Me	Lobo
	10/14	2	2	30.	Use Me	Bill Withers
	7/8	1	2	31.	Outa-Space	Billy Preston
	10/28	1	2	32.	Burning Love	Elvis Presley
	3/11	3	3	33.	The Lion Sleeps Tonight	Robert John
	8/5	2	3	34.	(If Loving You Is Wrong) I Don't Want To Be Right	Luther Ingram
	2/26	2	3	35.	Precious And Few	Climax
	12/23	2	3	36.	You Ought To Be With Me	Al Green
	9/2	2	3	37.	I'm Still In Love With You	Al Green
	12/9	2	3	38.	If You Don't Know Me By Now	Harold Melvin & The Bluenotes
	11/18	2	3	39.	I'll Be Around	The Spinners
	9/23	2	3	40.	Saturday In The Park	Chicago

TOP 40 HITS   1973

RANK	PEAK DATE	PEAK WKS	PEAK POS		TITLE	ARTIST
146	2/24	5	1	1.	Killing Me Softly With His Song	Roberta Flack
189	4/21	4	1	2.	Tie A Yellow Ribbon Round The Ole Oak Tree	Dawn Feat. Tony Orlando
215	6/2	4	1	3.	My Love	Paul McCartney & Wings
279	1/6	3	1	4.	You're So Vain	Carly Simon
302	2/3	3	1	5.	Crocodile Rock	Elton John
404	9/8	2	1	6.	Let's Get It On	Marvin Gaye
431	11/10	2	1	7.	Keep On Truckin' (Part 1)	Eddie Kendricks
486	7/21	2	1	8.	Bad, Bad Leroy Brown	Jim Croce
489	12/1	2	1	9.	Top Of The World	Carpenters
490	10/27	2	1	10.	Midnight Train To Georgia	Gladys Knight & The Pips
497	8/25	2	1	11.	Brother Louie	Stories
500	7/7	2	1	12.	Will It Go Round In Circles	Billy Preston
502	10/6	2	1	13.	Half-Breed	Cher
543	4/7	2	1	14.	The Night The Lights Went Out In Georgia	Vicki Lawrence
557	12/29	2	1	15.	Time In A Bottle	Jim Croce
577	12/15	2	1	16.	The Most Beautiful Girl	Charlie Rich
616	8/4	2	1	17.	The Morning After	Maureen McGovern
735	8/18	1	1	18.	Touch Me In The Morning	Diana Ross
756	9/15	1	1	19.	Delta Dawn	Helen Reddy
804	5/26	1	1	20.	Frankenstein	The Edgar Winter Group
825	5/19	1	1	21.	You Are The Sunshine Of My Life	Stevie Wonder
828	10/20	1	1	22.	Angie	The Rolling Stones
855	6/30	1	1	23.	Give Me Love - (Give Me Peace On Earth)	George Harrison
904	9/29	1	1	24.	We're An American Band	Grand Funk
906	1/27	1	1	25.	Superstition	Stevie Wonder
910	3/24	1	1	26.	Love Train	O'Jays
921	11/24	1	1	27.	Photograph	Ringo Starr
	2/24	4	2	28.	Dueling Banjos	Eric Weissberg & Steve Mandell
	12/8	3	2	29.	Goodbye Yellow Brick Road	Elton John
	8/11	3	2	30.	Live And Let Die	Wings
	6/16	2	2	31.	Playground In My Mind	Clint Holmes
	7/7	2	2	32.	Kodachrome	Paul Simon
	4/7	2	2	33.	Neither One Of Us (Wants To Be The First To Say Goodbye)	Gladys Knight & The Pips
	4/28	2	2	34.	The Cisco Kid	War
	10/6	1	2	35.	Loves Me Like A Rock	Paul Simon
	6/2	1	2	36.	Daniel	Elton John
	10/13	1	2	37.	Ramblin Man	The Allman Brothers Band
	7/28	1	2	38.	Yesterday Once More	Carpenters
	3/31	1	2	39.	Also Sprach Zarathustra (2001)	Deodato
	5/5	3	3	40.	Little Willy	The Sweet

RANK	PEAK DATE	PEAK WKS	PEAK POS		TITLE	ARTIST
297	2/2	3	1	1.	The Way We Were	Barbra Streisand
315	3/2	3	1	2.	Seasons In The Sun	Terry Jacks
334	5/18	3	1	3.	The Streak	Ray Stevens
382	8/24	3	1	4.	(You're) Having My Baby	Paul Anka with Odia Coates
514	12/7	2	1	5.	Kung Fu Fighting	Carl Douglas
554	6/15	2	1	6.	Billy, Don't Be A Hero	Bo Donaldson & The Heywoods
564	7/27	2	1	7.	Annie's Song	John Denver
589	5/4	2	1	8.	The Loco-Motion	Grand Funk
594	4/20	2	1	9.	TSOP (The Sound Of Philadelphia)	MFSB with The Three Degrees
612	11/23	2	1	10.	I Can Help	Billy Swan
630	7/13	2	1	11.	Rock Your Baby	George McCrae
631	10/5	2	1	12.	I Honestly Love You	Olivia Newton-John
707	4/13	1	1	13.	Bennie And The Jets	Elton John
737	1/12	1	1	14.	The Joker	Steve Miller Band
747	10/26	1	1	15.	Then Came You	Dionne Warwicke & Spinners
778	2/9	1	1	16.	Love's Theme	Love Unlimited Orchestra
779	1/19	1	1	17.	Show And Tell	Al Wilson
805	11/2	1	1	18.	You Haven't Done Nothin	Stevie Wonder
808	10/19	1	1	19.	Nothing From Nothing	Billy Preston
811	4/6	1	1	20.	Hooked On A Feeling	Blue Swede
822	3/30	1	1	21.	Sunshine On My Shoulders	John Denver
823	6/8	1	1	22.	Band On The Run	Paul McCartney & Wings
838	1/26	1	1	23.	You're Sixteen	Ringo Starr
848	6/29	1	1	24.	Sundown	Gordon Lightfoot
900	9/28	1	1	25.	Rock Me Gently	Andy Kim
903	12/28	1	1	26.	Angie Baby	Helen Reddy
907	8/10	1	1	27.	Feel Like Makin' Love	Roberta Flack
915	12/21	1	1	28.	Cat's In The Cradle	Harry Chapin
922	3/23	1	1	29.	Dark Lady	Cher
928	8/17	1	1	30.	The Night Chicago Died	Paper Lace
952	11/9	1	1	31.	You Ain't Seen Nothing Yet	Bachman-Turner Overdrive
957	7/6	1	1	32.	Rock The Boat	The Hues Corporation
959	9/14	1	1	33.	I Shot The Sheriff	Eric Clapton
972	9/21	1	1	34.	Can't Get Enough Of Your Love, Babe	Barry White
974	11/16	1	1	35.	Whatever Gets You Thru The Night	John Lennon
	5/18	2	2	36.	Dancing Machine	The Jackson 5
	6/15	2	2	37.	You Make Me Feel Brand New	The Stylistics
	11/16	2	2	38.	Do It ('Til You're Satisfied)	B.T. Express
	3/9	2	2	39.	Boogie Down	Eddie Kendricks
	7/27	2	2	40.	Don't Let The Sun Go Down On Me	Elton John

RANK	PEAK DATE	PEAK WKS	PEAK POS	TITLE	ARTIST
243	6/21	4	1	1. Love Will Keep Us Together	The Captain & Tennille
360	11/29	3	1	2. Fly, Robin, Fly	Silver Convention
364	11/1	3	1	3. Island Girl	Elton John
383	5/3	3	1	4. He Don't Love You (Like I Love You)	Tony Orlando & Dawn
384	10/11	3	1	5. Bad Blood	Neil Sedaka
441	9/6	2	1	6. Rhinestone Cowboy	Glen Campbell
446	4/12	2	1	7. Philadelphia Freedom	The Elton John Band
464	11/22	2	1	8. That's The Way (I Like It)	KC & The Sunshine Band
515	8/9	2	1	9. Jive Talkin'	Bee Gees
588	9/20	2	1	10. Fame	David Bowie
620	1/4	2	1	11. Lucy In The Sky With Diamonds	Elton John
684	8/2	1	1	12. One Of These Nights	Eagles
743	5/31	1	1	13. Before The Next Teardrop Falls	Freddy Fender
749	3/22	1	1	14. My Eyes Adored You	Frankie Valli
763	4/5	1	1	15. Lovin' You	Minnie Riperton
791	2/1	1	1	16. Laughter In The Rain	Neil Sedaka
809	4/26	1	1	17. (Hey Won't You Play) Another Somebody Done Somebody Wrong Song	B.J. Thomas
824	3/29	1	1	18. Lady Marmalade	LaBelle
826	2/22	1	1	19. Pick Up The Pieces	AWB
834	7/26	1	1	20. The Hustle	Van McCoy
835	3/15	1	1	21. Black Water	The Doobie Brothers
839	12/27	1	1	22. Let's Do It Again	The Staple Singers
850	3/8	1	1	23. Have You Never Been Mellow	Olivia Newton-John
853	7/19	1	1	24. Listen To What The Man Said	Wings
889	3/1	1	1	25. Best Of My Love	The Eagles
919	8/23	1	1	26. Fallin' In Love	Hamilton, Joe Frank & Reynolds
941	6/7	1	1	27. Thank God I'm A Country Boy	John Denver
942	5/24	1	1	28. Shining Star	Earth, Wind & Fire
953	1/25	1	1	29. Please Mr. Postman	Carpenters
954	1/18	1	1	30. Mandy	Barry Manilow
958	2/15	1	1	31. You're No Good	Linda Ronstadt
967	9/27	1	1	32. I'm Sorry	John Denver
968	2/8	1	1	33. Fire	Ohio Players
969	6/14	1	1	34. Sister Golden Hair	America
971	8/30	1	1	35. Get Down Tonight	KC & The Sunshine Band
	10/11	4	2	36. Calypso	John Denver
	7/26	3	2	37. I'm Not In Love	10cc
	6/21	2	2	38. When Will I Be Loved	Linda Ronstadt
	1/4	2	2	39. You're The First, The Last, My Everything	Barry White
	11/8	2	2	40. Lyin' Eyes	The Eagles

RANK	PEAK DATE	PEAK WKS	PEAK POS	TITLE	ARTIST
48	11/13	8	1	1. Tonight's The Night (Gonna Be Alright)	Rod Stewart
128	5/22	5	1	2. Silly Love Songs	Wings
231	8/7	4	1	3. Don't Go Breaking My Heart	Elton John & Kiki Dee
234	4/3	4	1	4. Disco Lady	Johnnie Taylor
282	9/18	3	1	5. Play That Funky Music	Wild Cherry
378	3/13	3	1	6. December, 1963 (Oh, What a Night)	The Four Seasons
379	2/7	3	1	7. 50 Ways To Leave Your Lover	Paul Simon
442	7/24	2	1	8. Kiss And Say Goodbye	Manhattans
447	10/23	2	1	9. If You Leave Me Now	Chicago
460	5/29	2	1	10. Love Hangover	Diana Ross
505	7/10	2	1	11. Afternoon Delight	Starland Vocal Band
667	9/11	1	1	12. (Shake, Shake, Shake) Shake Your Booty	KC & The Sunshine Band
671	10/9	1	1	13. A Fifth Of Beethoven	Walter Murphy
676	10/16	1	1	14. Disco Duck (Part 1)	Rick Dees & His Cast Of Idiots
679	1/17	1	1	15. I Write The Songs	Barry Manilow
686	1/31	1	1	16. Love Rollercoaster	Ohio Players
788	5/15	1	1	17. Boogie Fever	Sylvers
827	1/24	1	1	18. Theme From Mahogany (Do You Know Where You're Going To)	Diana Ross
831	9/4	1	1	19. You Should Be Dancing	Bee Gees
833	5/1	1	1	20. Let Your Love Flow	Bellamy Brothers
851	1/10	1	1	21. Convoy	C.W. McCall
854	5/8	1	1	22. Welcome Back	John Sebastian
865	3/6	1	1	23. Love Machine (Part 1)	The Miracles
912	2/28	1	1	24. Theme From S.W.A.T.	Rhythm Heritage
917	1/3	1	1	25. Saturday Night	Bay City Rollers
943	11/6	1	1	26. Rock'n Me	Steve Miller
	12/4	3	2	27. The Rubberband Man	Spinners
	6/12	3	2	28. Get Up And Boogie (That's Right)	Silver Convention
	3/27	3	2	29. Dream Weaver	Gary Wright
	3/6	3	2	30. All By Myself	Eric Carmen
	9/25	2	2	31. I'd Really Love To See You Tonight	England Dan & John Ford Coley
	5/1	2	2	32. Right Back Where We Started From	Maxine Nightingale
	9/4	2	2	33. You'll Never Find Another Love Like Mine	Lou Rawls
	7/31	2	2	34. Love Is Alive	Gary Wright
	2/7	2	2	35. Love To Love You Baby	Donna Summer
	11/20	2	2	36. The Wreck Of The Edmund Fitzgerald	Gordon Lightfoot
	11/20	4	3	37. Love So Right	Bee Gees
	6/12	4	3	38. Misty Blue	Dorothy Moore
	8/14	4	3	39. Let 'Em In	Wings
	2/7	3	3	40. You Sexy Thing	Hot Chocolate

RANK	PEAK DATE	PEAK WKS	PEAK POS		TITLE	ARTIST
23	10/15	10	1	1.	You Light Up My Life	Debby Boone
121	8/20	5	1	2.	Best Of My Love	Emotions
164	7/30	4	1	3.	I Just Want To Be Your Everything	Andy Gibb
252	12/24	3	1	4.	How Deep Is Your Love	Bee Gees
259	3/5	3	1	5.	Love Theme From "A Star Is Born" (Evergreen)	Barbra Streisand
329	5/21	3	1	6.	Sir Duke	Stevie Wonder
428	2/5	2	1	7.	Torn Between Two Lovers	Mary MacGregor
592	3/26	2	1	8.	Rich Girl	Daryl Hall & John Oates
600	10/1	2	1	9.	Star Wars Theme/Cantina Band	Meco
711	6/25	1	1	10.	Got To Give It Up (Pt. I)	Marvin Gaye
715	1/29	1	1	11.	Car Wash	Rose Royce
728	1/8	1	1	12.	You Don't Have To Be A Star (To Be In My Show)	Marilyn McCoo & Billy Davis, Jr.
732	4/23	1	1	13.	Don't Leave Me This Way	Thelma Houston
733	1/15	1	1	14.	You Make Me Feel Like Dancing	Leo Sayer
739	4/9	1	1	15.	Dancing Queen	Abba
744	4/30	1	1	16.	Southern Nights	Glen Campbell
745	2/19	1	1	17.	Blinded By The Light	Manfred Mann's Earth Band
746	5/7	1	1	18.	Hotel California	Eagles
748	1/22	1	1	19.	I Wish	Stevie Wonder
761	7/2	1	1	20.	Gonna Fly Now	Bill Conti
776	7/9	1	1	21.	Undercover Angel	Alan O'Day
802	5/14	1	1	22.	When I Need You	Leo Sayer
819	4/16	1	1	23.	Don't Give Up On Us	David Soul
821	6/18	1	1	24.	Dreams	Fleetwood Mac
829	2/26	1	1	25.	New Kid In Town	Eagles
830	7/16	1	1	26.	Da Doo Ron Ron	Shaun Cassidy
866	6/11	1	1	27.	I'm Your Boogie Man	KC & The Sunshine Band
947	7/23	1	1	28.	Looks Like We Made It	Barry Manilow
	11/26	3	2	29.	Don't It Make My Brown Eyes Blue	Crystal Gayle
	10/22	3	2	30.	Nobody Does It Better	Carly Simon
	10/1	3	2	31.	Keep It Comin' Love	KC & The Sunshine Band
	7/30	3	2	32.	I'm In You	Peter Frampton
	11/12	2	2	33.	Boogie Nights	Heatwave
	3/12	2	2	34.	Fly Like An Eagle	Steve Miller
	9/17	2	2	35.	Float On	The Floaters
	9/10	1	2	36.	(Your Love Has Lifted Me) Higher And Higher	Rita Coolidge
	12/17	4	3	37.	Blue Bayou	Linda Ronstadt
	1/29	2	3	38.	Dazz	Brick
	10/22	2	3	39.	That's Rock 'N' Roll	Shaun Cassidy
	9/24	2	3	40.	Don't Stop	Fleetwood Mac

TOP 40 HITS   1978

RANK	PEAK DATE	PEAK WKS	PEAK POS		TITLE	ARTIST
46	3/18	8	1	1.	Night Fever	Bee Gees
60	6/17	7	1	2.	Shadow Dancing	Andy Gibb
84	12/9	6	1	3.	Le Freak	Chic
172	2/4	4	1	4.	Stayin' Alive	Bee Gees
186	9/30	4	1	5.	Kiss You All Over	Exile
268	9/9	3	1	6.	Boogie Oogie Oogie	A Taste Of Honey
284	1/14	3	1	7.	Baby Come Back	Player
300	11/11	3	1	8.	MacArthur Park	Donna Summer
411	3/4	2	1	9.	(Love Is) Thicker Than Water	Andy Gibb
415	8/12	2	1	10.	Three Times A Lady	Commodores
432	12/2	2	1	11.	You Don't Bring Me Flowers	Barbra & Neil
492	8/26	2	1	12.	Grease	Frankie Valli
513	5/20	2	1	13.	With A Little Luck	Wings
677	5/13	1	1	14.	If I Can't Have You	Yvonne Elliman
691	10/28	1	1	15.	Hot Child In The City	Nick Gilder
698	6/10	1	1	16.	You're The One That I Want	John Travolta & Olivia Newton-John
705	8/5	1	1	17.	Miss You	The Rolling Stones
730	11/4	1	1	18.	You Needed Me	Anne Murray
771	6/3	1	1	19.	Too Much, Too Little, Too Late	Johnny Mathis/Deniece Williams
996	6/24	6	2	20.	Baker Street	Gerry Rafferty
	1/28	3	2	21.	Short People	Randy Newman
	5/13	2	2	22.	The Closer I Get To You	Roberta Flack/Donny Hathaway
	11/18	2	2	23.	Double Vision	Foreigner
	4/1	3	3	24.	Lay Down Sally	Eric Clapton
	4/22	3	3	25.	Can't Smile Without You	Barry Manilow
	11/18	3	3	26.	How Much I Feel	Ambrosia
	3/18	2	3	27.	Emotion	Samantha Sang
	2/18	2	3	28.	Just The Way You Are	Billy Joel
	3/4	2	3	29.	Sometimes When We Touch	Dan Hill
	9/23	2	3	30.	Hopelessly Devoted To You	Olivia Newton-John
	7/8	2	3	31.	Take A Chance On Me	Abba
	9/9	2	3	32.	Hot Blooded	Foreigner
	8/12	2	3	33.	Last Dance	Donna Summer
	10/28	2	3	34.	Reminiscing	Little River Band
	6/24	2	3	35.	It's A Heartache	Bonnie Tyler
	1/14	2	3	36.	Here You Come Again	Dolly Parton
	2/4	3	4	37.	We Are The Champions	Queen
	1/14	3	4	38.	You're In My Heart (The Final Acclaim)	Rod Stewart
	12/9	2	4	39.	I Just Wanna Stop	Gino Vannelli
	7/8	2	4	40.	Use Ta Be My Girl	The O'Jays

TOP 40 HITS   1979

RANK	PEAK DATE	PEAK WKS	PEAK POS		TITLE	ARTIST
96	8/25	6	1	1.	My Sharona	The Knack
133	7/14	5	1	2.	Bad Girls	Donna Summer
185	2/10	4	1	3.	Da Ya Think I'm Sexy?	Rod Stewart
198	5/5	4	1	4.	Reunited	Peaches & Herb
258	6/2	3	1	5.	Hot Stuff	Donna Summer
260	3/10	3	1	6.	I Will Survive	Gloria Gaynor
286	12/22	3	1	7.	Escape (The Pina Colada Song)	Rupert Holmes
416	6/30	2	1	8.	Ring My Bell	Anita Ward
421	12/8	2	1	9.	Babe	Styx
448	1/6	2	1	10.	Too Much Heaven	Bee Gees
452	10/20	2	1	11.	Rise	Herb Alpert
459	3/24	2	1	12.	Tragedy	Bee Gees
471	11/24	2	1	13.	No More Tears (Enough Is Enough)	Barbra Streisand/Donna Summer
656	11/17	1	1	14.	Still	Commodores
689	11/3	1	1	15.	Pop Muzik	M
690	10/6	1	1	16.	Sad Eyes	Robert John
717	4/14	1	1	17.	What A Fool Believes	The Doobie Brothers
718	8/18	1	1	18.	Good Times	Chic
722	11/10	1	1	19.	Heartache Tonight	Eagles
798	4/28	1	1	20.	Heart Of Glass	Blondie
884	4/21	1	1	21.	Knock On Wood	Amii Stewart
914	10/13	1	1	22.	Don't Stop 'Til You Get Enough	Michael Jackson
948	6/9	1	1	23.	Love You Inside Out	Bee Gees
	2/3	3	2	24.	Y.M.C.A.	Village People
	11/10	2	2	25.	Dim All The Lights	Donna Summer
	9/15	2	2	26.	After The Love Has Gone	Earth, Wind & Fire
	2/24	2	2	27.	Fire	Pointer Sisters
	6/16	2	2	28.	We Are Family	Sister Sledge
	8/11	4	3	29.	The Main Event/Fight	Barbra Streisand
	1/6	3	3	30.	My Life	Billy Joel
	2/17	2	3	31.	A Little More Love	Olivia Newton-John
	9/15	2	3	32.	The Devil Went Down To Georgia	The Charlie Daniels Band
	5/19	2	3	33.	In The Navy	Village People
	5/5	1	3	34.	Music Box Dancer	Frank Mills
	12/22	4	4	35.	Send One Your Love	Stevie Wonder
	3/17	3	4	36.	Heaven Knows	Donna Summer with Brooklyn Dreams
	5/12	2	4	37.	Stumblin' In	Suzi Quatro & Chris Norman
	10/13	2	4	38.	Sail On	Commodores
	4/7	2	4	39.	Sultans Of Swing	Dire Straits
	6/16	2	4	40.	Just When I Needed You Most	Randy Vanwarmer

TOP 40 HITS   1980

RANK	PEAK DATE	PEAK WKS	PEAK POS	TITLE	ARTIST
89	11/15	6	1	1. Lady	Kenny Rogers
94	4/19	6	1	2. Call Me	Blondie
116	12/27	5	1	3. (Just Like) Starting Over	John Lennon
170	9/6	4	1	4. Upside Down	Diana Ross
182	3/22	4	1	5. Another Brick In The Wall (Part II)	Pink Floyd
187	2/23	4	1	6. Crazy Little Thing Called Love	Queen
210	1/19	4	1	7. Rock With You	Michael Jackson
211	8/2	4	1	8. Magic	Olivia Newton-John
213	5/31	4	1	9. Funkytown	Lipps, Inc.
255	10/4	3	1	10. Another One Bites The Dust	Queen
271	10/25	3	1	11. Woman In Love	Barbra Streisand
275	6/28	3	1	12. Coming Up (Live at Glasgow)	Paul McCartney & Wings
413	7/19	2	1	13. It's Still Rock And Roll To Me	Billy Joel
648	2/16	1	1	14. Do That To Me One More Time	The Captain & Tennille
665	1/5	1	1	15. Please Don't Go	K.C. & The Sunshine Band
816	8/30	1	1	16. Sailing	Christopher Cross
	12/6	5	2	17. More Than I Can Say	Leo Sayer
	9/13	4	2	18. All Out Of Love	Air Supply
	4/26	4	2	19. Ride Like The Wind	Christopher Cross
	3/29	2	2	20. Working My Way Back To You/Forgive Me, Girl	Spinners
	3/1	2	2	21. Yes, I'm Ready	Teri DeSario with K.C.
	3/15	2	2	22. Longer	Dan Fogelberg
	7/19	4	3	23. Little Jeannie	Elton John
	1/26	4	3	24. Coward Of The County	Kenny Rogers
	5/3	4	3	25. Lost In Love	Air Supply
	6/28	3	3	26. The Rose	Bette Midler
	6/7	3	3	27. Biggest Part Of Me	Ambrosia
	11/15	3	3	28. The Wanderer	Donna Summer
	10/25	3	3	29. He's So Shy	Pointer Sisters
	9/6	2	3	30. Emotional Rescue	The Rolling Stones
	8/16	2	3	31. Take Your Time (Do It Right) Part 1	The S.O.S. Band
	3/8	4	4	32. Desire	Andy Gibb
	2/2	4	4	33. Cruisin'	Smokey Robinson
	4/19	4	4	34. With You I'm Born Again	Billy Preston & Syreeta
	7/19	3	4	35. Cupid/I've Loved You For A Long Time	Spinners
	5/24	3	4	36. Don't Fall In Love With A Dreamer	Kenny Rogers with Kim Carnes
	9/27	2	4	37. Give Me The Night	George Benson
	9/13	2	4	38. Fame	Irene Cara
	12/27	5	5	39. Hungry Heart	Bruce Springsteen
	12/6	3	5	40. Master Blaster (Jammin')	Stevie Wonder

RANK	PEAK DATE	PEAK WKS	PEAK POS		TITLE	ARTIST
21	11/21	10	1	1.	Physical	Olivia Newton-John
30	5/16	9	1	2.	Bette Davis Eyes	Kim Carnes
33	8/15	9	1	3.	Endless Love	Diana Ross & Lionel Richie
267	10/17	3	1	4.	Arthur's Theme (Best That You Can Do)	Christopher Cross
313	4/11	3	1	5.	Kiss On My List	Daryl Hall & John Oates
408	8/1	2	1	6.	Jessie's Girl	Rick Springfield
439	2/28	2	1	7.	I Love A Rainy Night	Eddie Rabbitt
440	2/21	2	1	8.	9 To 5	Dolly Parton
445	11/7	2	1	9.	Private Eyes	Daryl Hall & John Oates
504	3/28	2	1	10.	Rapture	Blondie
527	2/7	2	1	11.	Celebration	Kool & The Gang
581	5/2	2	1	12.	Morning Train (Nine To Five)	Sheena Easton
675	1/31	1	1	13.	The Tide Is High	Blondie
688	3/21	1	1	14.	Keep On Loving You	REO Speedwagon
752	6/20	1	1	15.	Medley	Stars on 45
759	7/25	1	1	16.	The One That You Love	Air Supply
977	11/28	10	2	17.	Waiting For A Girl Like You	Foreigner
	3/21	3	2	18.	Woman	John Lennon
	10/31	3	2	19.	Start Me Up	The Rolling Stones
	8/29	3	2	20.	Slow Hand	Pointer Sisters
	5/2	3	2	21.	Just The Two Of Us	Grover Washington, Jr. (with Bill Withers)
	1/10	3	2	22.	Love On The Rocks	Neil Diamond
	5/23	3	2	23.	Being With You	Smokey Robinson
	7/4	3	2	24.	All Those Years Ago	George Harrison
	9/19	2	2	25.	Queen Of Hearts	Juice Newton
	8/15	2	2	26.	Theme From "Greatest American Hero" (Believe It or Not)	Joey Scarbury
	9/5	6	3	27.	Stop Draggin' My Heart Around	Stevie Nicks (with Tom Petty & The Heartbreakers)
	12/19	5	3	28.	Let's Groove	Earth, Wind & Fire
	3/21	4	3	29.	The Best Of Times	Styx
	6/13	3	3	30.	Sukiyaki	A Taste Of Honey
	8/15	2	3	31.	I Don't Need You	Kenny Rogers
	1/10	2	3	32.	Guilty	Barbra Streisand & Barry Gibb
	12/5	2	3	33.	Every Little Thing She Does Is Magic	The Police
	9/5	4	4	34.	Urgent	Foreigner
	5/2	4	4	35.	Angel Of The Morning	Juice Newton
	10/17	4	4	36.	For Your Eyes Only	Sheena Easton
	12/5	3	4	37.	Oh No	Commodores
	10/3	2	4	38.	Who's Crying Now	Journey
	6/20	2	4	39.	A Woman Needs Love (Just Like You Do)	Ray Parker Jr. & Raydio
	9/5	5	5	40.	(There's) No Gettin' Over Me	Ronnie Milsap

TOP 40 HITS   1982

RANK	PEAK DATE	PEAK WKS	PEAK POS	TITLE	ARTIST
63	3/20	7	1	1. I Love Rock 'N Roll	Joan Jett & The Blackhearts
64	5/15	7	1	2. Ebony And Ivory	Paul McCartney/Stevie Wonder
86	7/24	6	1	3. Eye Of The Tiger	Survivor
93	2/6	6	1	4. Centerfold	The J. Geils Band
176	12/18	4	1	5. Maneater	Daryl Hall & John Oates
196	10/2	4	1	6. Jack & Diane	John Cougar
263	7/3	3	1	7. Don't You Want Me	The Human League
350	11/6	3	1	8. Up Where We Belong	Joe Cocker & Jennifer Warnes
399	9/4	2	1	9. Abracadabra	The Steve Miller Band
410	9/11	2	1	10. Hard To Say I'm Sorry	Chicago
436	11/27	2	1	11. Truly	Lionel Richie
661	1/30	1	1	12. I Can't Go For That (No Can Do)	Daryl Hall & John Oates
673	12/11	1	1	13. Mickey	Toni Basil
693	10/30	1	1	14. Who Can It Be Now?	Men At Work
709	5/8	1	1	15. Chariots Of Fire	Vangelis
995	2/27	6	2	16. Open Arms	Journey
	7/3	5	2	17. Rosanna	Toto
	8/7	4	2	18. Hurts So Good	John Cougar
	5/22	4	2	19. Don't Talk To Strangers	Rick Springfield
	11/27	3	2	20. Gloria	Laura Branigan
	4/10	3	2	21. We Got The Beat	Go-Go's
	11/6	4	3	22. Heart Attack	Olivia Newton-John
	10/16	3	3	23. Eye In The Sky	The Alan Parsons Project
	5/22	3	3	24. I've Never Been To Me	Charlene
	2/13	2	3	25. Harden My Heart	Quarterflash
	7/24	7	4	26. Hold Me	Fleetwood Mac
	4/10	4	4	27. Freeze-Frame	The J. Geils Band
	3/20	3	4	28. That Girl	Stevie Wonder
	5/22	3	4	29. 867-5309/Jenny	Tommy Tutone
	2/27	3	4	30. Shake It Up	The Cars
	10/23	3	4	31. I Keep Forgettin' (Every Time You're Near)	Michael McDonald
	6/26	3	4	32. Heat Of The Moment	Asia
	6/12	2	4	33. The Other Woman	Ray Parker Jr.
	11/13	4	5	34. Heartlight	Neil Diamond
	6/12	3	5	35. Always On My Mind	Willie Nelson
	9/18	3	5	36. You Should Hear How She Talks About You	Melissa Manchester
	4/3	3	5	37. Make A Move On Me	Olivia Newton-John
	9/4	2	5	38. Even The Nights Are Better	Air Supply
	3/20	2	5	39. Sweet Dreams	Air Supply
	7/17	2	5	40. Let It Whip	Dazz Band

149

TOP 40 HITS   1983

RANK	PEAK DATE	PEAK WKS	PEAK POS		TITLE	ARTIST
44	7/9	8	1	1.	Every Breath You Take	The Police
67	3/5	7	1	2.	Billie Jean	Michael Jackson
87	5/28	6	1	3.	Flashdance...What A Feeling	Irene Cara
90	12/10	6	1	4.	Say Say Say	Paul McCartney/Michael Jackson
175	11/12	4	1	5.	All Night Long (All Night)	Lionel Richie
188	10/1	4	1	6.	Total Eclipse Of The Heart	Bonnie Tyler
194	1/15	4	1	7.	Down Under	Men At Work
281	4/30	3	1	8.	Beat It	Michael Jackson
409	10/29	2	1	9.	Islands In The Stream	Kenny Rogers with Dolly Parton
438	2/19	2	1	10.	Baby, Come To Me	Patti Austin with James Ingram
450	9/10	2	1	11.	Maniac	Michael Sembello
683	5/21	1	1	12.	Let's Dance	David Bowie
694	9/3	1	1	13.	Sweet Dreams (Are Made of This)	Eurythmics
792	9/24	1	1	14.	Tell Her About It	Billy Joel
867	2/5	1	1	15.	Africa	Toto
877	4/23	1	1	16.	Come On Eileen	Dexys Midnight Runners
	7/2	5	2	17.	Electric Avenue	Eddy Grant
	12/17	4	2	18.	Say It Isn't So	Daryl Hall & John Oates
	2/26	4	2	19.	Shame On The Moon	Bob Seger
	1/8	3	2	20.	The Girl Is Mine	Michael Jackson/Paul McCartney
	3/26	3	2	21.	Do You Really Want To Hurt Me	Culture Club
	10/8	3	2	22.	Making Love Out Of Nothing At All	Air Supply
	6/18	2	2	23.	Time (Clock Of The Heart)	Culture Club
	5/7	1	2	24.	Jeopardy	Greg Kihn Band
	11/12	5	3	25.	Uptown Girl	Billy Joel
	9/10	4	3	26.	The Safety Dance	Men Without Hats
	1/29	3	3	27.	Sexual Healing	Marvin Gaye
	1/8	3	3	28.	Dirty Laundry	Don Henley
	3/26	3	3	29.	Hungry Like The Wolf	Duran Duran
	8/6	3	3	30.	She Works Hard For The Money	Donna Summer
	12/24	3	3	31.	Union Of The Snake	Duran Duran
	2/26	3	3	32.	Stray Cat Strut	Stray Cats
	4/16	2	3	33.	Mr. Roboto	Styx
	10/8	2	3	34.	King Of Pain	The Police
	6/4	1	3	35.	Overkill	Men At Work
	7/9	4	4	36.	Never Gonna Let You Go	Sergio Mendes
	10/8	4	4	37.	True	Spandau Ballet
	9/3	2	4	38.	Puttin' On The Ritz	Taco
	3/26	2	4	39.	You Are	Lionel Richie
	11/5	1	4	40.	One Thing Leads To Another	The Fixx

TOP 40 HITS   1984

RANK	PEAK DATE	PEAK WKS	PEAK POS	TITLE	ARTIST
105	12/22	6	1	1. Like A Virgin	Madonna
124	7/7	5	1	2. When Doves Cry	Prince
132	2/25	5	1	3. Jump	Van Halen
274	3/31	3	1	4. Footloose	Kenny Loggins
280	9/1	3	1	5. What's Love Got To Do With It	Tina Turner
285	4/21	3	1	6. Against All Odds (Take A Look At Me Now)	Phil Collins
288	10/13	3	1	7. I Just Called To Say I Love You	Stevie Wonder
291	8/11	3	1	8. Ghostbusters	Ray Parker Jr.
299	2/4	3	1	9. Karma Chameleon	Culture Club
317	11/17	3	1	10. Wake Me Up Before You Go-Go	Wham!
425	5/12	2	1	11. Hello	Lionel Richie
426	1/21	2	1	12. Owner Of A Lonely Heart	Yes
449	12/8	2	1	13. Out Of Touch	Daryl Hall/John Oates
454	6/9	2	1	14. Time After Time	Cyndi Lauper
455	5/26	2	1	15. Let's Hear It For The Boy	Deniece Williams
456	9/29	2	1	16. Let's Go Crazy	Prince & the Revolution
494	6/23	2	1	17. The Reflex	Duran Duran
531	11/3	2	1	18. Caribbean Queen (No More Love On The Run)	Billy Ocean
699	9/22	1	1	19. Missing You	John Waite
	6/30	4	2	20. Dancing In The Dark	Bruce Springsteen
	12/15	4	2	21. The Wild Boys	Duran Duran
	3/24	3	2	22. Somebody's Watching Me	Rockwell
	3/10	2	2	23. Girls Just Want To Have Fun	Cyndi Lauper
	11/17	2	2	24. Purple Rain	Prince & the Revolution
	2/11	1	2	25. Joanna	Kool & The Gang
	3/3	1	2	26. 99 Luftballons	Nena
	11/24	3	3	27. I Feel For You	Chaka Khan
	9/8	3	3	28. She Bop	Cyndi Lauper
	1/28	3	3	29. Talking In Your Sleep	The Romantics
	9/29	3	3	30. Drive	The Cars
	8/4	3	3	31. State Of Shock	Jacksons
	7/7	2	3	32. Jump (For My Love)	Pointer Sisters
	5/5	2	3	33. Hold Me Now	Thompson Twins
	8/25	2	3	34. Stuck On You	Lionel Richie
	10/20	2	3	35. Hard Habit To Break	Chicago
	6/9	1	3	36. Oh Sherrie	Steve Perry
	3/31	2	4	37. Here Comes The Rain Again	Eurythmics
	6/30	2	4	38. Self Control	Laura Branigan
	7/14	2	4	39. Eyes Without A Face	Billy Idol
	3/3	2	4	40. Thriller	Michael Jackson

TOP 40 HITS   1985

RANK	PEAK DATE	PEAK WKS	PEAK POS		TITLE	ARTIST
212	12/21	4	1	1.	Say You, Say Me	Lionel Richie
236	4/13	4	1	2.	We Are The World	USA for Africa
298	2/16	3	1	3.	Careless Whisper	Wham!
320	3/9	3	1	4.	Can't Fight This Feeling	REO Speedwagon
327	9/21	3	1	5.	Money For Nothing	Dire Straits
358	8/3	3	1	6.	Shout	Tears For Fears
453	12/7	2	1	7.	Broken Wings	Mr. Mister
487	2/2	2	1	8.	I Want To Know What Love Is	Foreigner
495	8/24	2	1	9.	The Power Of Love	Huey Lewis & The News
499	6/8	2	1	10.	Everybody Wants To Rule The World	Tears For Fears
532	11/16	2	1	11.	We Built This City	Starship
541	9/7	2	1	12.	St. Elmo's Fire (Man In Motion)	John Parr
591	5/25	2	1	13.	Everything She Wants	Wham!
593	6/22	2	1	14.	Heaven	Bryan Adams
604	7/13	2	1	15.	A View To A Kill	Duran Duran
610	3/30	2	1	16.	One More Night	Phil Collins
702	11/30	1	1	17.	Separate Lives	Phil Collins & Marilyn Martin
716	5/11	1	1	18.	Crazy For You	Madonna
738	7/27	1	1	19.	Everytime You Go Away	Paul Young
750	5/18	1	1	20.	Don't You (Forget About Me)	Simple Minds
753	11/2	1	1	21.	Part-Time Lover	Stevie Wonder
781	10/19	1	1	22.	Take On Me	A-Ha
786	10/26	1	1	23.	Saving All My Love For You	Whitney Houston
814	11/9	1	1	24.	Miami Vice Theme	Jan Hammer
893	7/6	1	1	25.	Sussudio	Phil Collins
896	10/12	1	1	26.	Oh Sheila	Ready For The World
	12/28	3	2	27.	Party All The Time	Eddie Murphy
	9/21	3	2	28.	Cherish	Kool & The Gang
	2/2	2	2	29.	Easy Lover	Philip Bailey/Phil Collins
	11/16	2	2	30.	You Belong To The City	Glenn Frey
	1/12	2	2	31.	All I Need	Jack Wagner
	3/23	2	2	32.	Material Girl	Madonna
	2/23	1	2	33.	Loverboy	Billy Ocean
	7/20	1	2	34.	Raspberry Beret	Prince & the Revolution
	3/16	1	2	35.	The Heat Is On	Glenn Frey
	9/14	1	2	36.	We Don't Need Another Hero (Thunderdome)	Tina Turner
	6/1	3	3	37.	Axel F	Harold Faltermeyer
	4/27	2	3	38.	Rhythm Of The Night	DeBarge
	12/28	2	3	39.	Alive & Kicking	Simple Minds
	1/19	2	3	40.	You're The Inspiration	Chicago

TOP 40 HITS   1986

RANK	PEAK DATE	PEAK WKS	PEAK POS	TITLE	ARTIST
195	1/18	4	1	1. That's What Friends Are For	Dionne & Friends
230	12/20	4	1	2. Walk Like An Egyptian	Bangles
351	6/14	3	1	3. On My Own	Patti LaBelle/Michael McDonald
355	5/17	3	1	4. Greatest Love Of All	Whitney Houston
359	9/20	3	1	5. Stuck With You	Huey Lewis & the News
361	3/29	3	1	6. Rock Me Amadeus	Falco
547	3/1	2	1	7. Kyrie	Mr. Mister
548	4/19	2	1	8. Kiss	Prince & The Revolution
549	8/16	2	1	9. Papa Don't Preach	Madonna
578	2/15	2	1	10. How Will I Know	Whitney Houston
587	8/2	2	1	11. Glory Of Love	Peter Cetera
601	10/11	2	1	12. When I Think Of You	Janet Jackson
608	10/25	2	1	13. True Colors	Cyndi Lauper
611	11/8	2	1	14. Amanda	Boston
740	12/13	1	1	15. The Way It Is	Bruce Hornsby & The Range
790	11/22	1	1	16. Human	Human League
796	5/3	1	1	17. Addicted To Love	Robert Palmer
799	7/5	1	1	18. There'll Be Sad Songs (To Make You Cry)	Billy Ocean
800	7/26	1	1	19. Sledgehammer	Peter Gabriel
801	5/10	1	1	20. West End Girls	Pet Shop Boys
815	9/13	1	1	21. Take My Breath Away	Berlin
818	3/15	1	1	22. Sara	Starship
832	9/6	1	1	23. Venus	Bananarama
874	12/6	1	1	24. The Next Time I Fall	Peter Cetera with Amy Grant
876	11/29	1	1	25. You Give Love A Bad Name	Bon Jovi
878	7/12	1	1	26. Holding Back The Years	Simply Red
879	8/30	1	1	27. Higher Love	Steve Winwood
898	3/22	1	1	28. These Dreams	Heart
901	6/7	1	1	29. Live To Tell	Madonna
918	7/19	1	1	30. Invisible Touch	Genesis
	10/18	3	2	31. Typical Male	Tina Turner
	9/13	2	2	32. Dancing On The Ceiling	Lionel Richie
	12/27	2	2	33. Everybody Have Fun Tonight	Wang Chung
	9/27	2	2	34. Friends And Lovers	Gloria Loring & Carl Anderson
	2/1	2	2	35. Burning Heart	Survivor
	7/26	1	2	36. Danger Zone	Kenny Loggins
	10/11	1	2	37. Don't Forget Me (When I'm Gone)	Glass Tiger
	2/15	1	2	38. When The Going Gets Tough, The Tough Get Going	Billy Ocean
	4/19	1	2	39. Manic Monday	Bangles
	11/8	1	2	40. I Didn't Mean To Turn You On	Robert Palmer

RANK	PEAK DATE	PEAK WKS	PEAK POS		TITLE	ARTIST
214	12/12	4	1	1.	Faith	George Michael
242	2/14	4	1	2.	Livin' On A Prayer	Bon Jovi
316	7/11	3	1	3.	Alone	Heart
328	5/16	3	1	4.	With Or Without You	U2
353	8/29	3	1	5.	La Bamba	Los Lobos
457	6/27	2	1	6.	I Wanna Dance With Somebody (Who Loves Me)	Whitney Houston
493	4/4	2	1	7.	Nothing's Gonna Stop Us Now	Starship
551	8/8	2	1	8.	I Still Haven't Found What I'm Looking For	U2
553	9/26	2	1	9.	Didn't We Almost Have It All	Whitney Houston
556	4/18	2	1	10.	I Knew You Were Waiting (For Me)	Aretha Franklin & George Michael
582	1/24	2	1	11.	At This Moment	Billy Vera & The Beaters
598	11/7	2	1	12.	I Think We're Alone Now	Tiffany
602	5/2	2	1	13.	(I Just) Died In Your Arms	Cutting Crew
613	3/21	2	1	14.	Lean On Me	Club Nouveau
629	10/24	2	1	15.	Bad	Michael Jackson
734	1/17	1	1	16.	Shake You Down	Gregory Abbott
793	10/10	1	1	17.	Here I Go Again	Whitesnake
797	6/13	1	1	18.	Always	Atlantic Starr
803	6/20	1	1	19.	Head To Toe	Lisa Lisa & Cult Jam
807	8/1	1	1	20.	Shakedown	Bob Seger
872	12/5	1	1	21.	Heaven Is A Place On Earth	Belinda Carlisle
873	11/28	1	1	22.	(I've Had) The Time Of My Life	Bill Medley & Jennifer Warnes
891	2/7	1	1	23.	Open Your Heart	Madonna
897	6/6	1	1	24.	You Keep Me Hangin' On	Kim Wilde
899	10/17	1	1	25.	Lost In Emotion	Lisa Lisa & Cult Jam
913	11/21	1	1	26.	Mony Mony "Live"	Billy Idol
925	3/14	1	1	27.	Jacob's Ladder	Huey Lewis & the News
929	8/22	1	1	28.	Who's That Girl	Madonna
931	9/19	1	1	29.	I Just Can't Stop Loving You	Michael Jackson
	5/2	4	2	30.	Looking For A New Love	Jody Watley
	10/24	3	2	31.	Causing A Commotion	Madonna
	1/17	2	2	32.	C'est La Vie	Robbie Nevil
	4/25	1	2	33.	Don't Dream It's Over	Crowded House
	12/19	1	2	34.	Is This Love	Whitesnake
	8/8	1	2	35.	I Want Your Sex	George Michael
	10/17	1	2	36.	U Got The Look	Prince
	1/10	1	2	37.	Notorious	Duran Duran
	2/21	1	2	38.	Keep Your Hands To Yourself	Georgia Satellites
	3/14	1	2	39.	Somewhere Out There	Linda Ronstadt & James Ingram
	3/21	1	2	40.	Let's Wait Awhile	Janet Jackson

TOP 40 HITS   1988

RANK	PEAK DATE	PEAK WKS	PEAK POS		TITLE	ARTIST
241	7/30	4	1	1.	Roll With It	Steve Winwood
318	12/24	3	1	2.	Every Rose Has Its Thorn	Poison
356	5/28	3	1	3.	One More Try	George Michael
485	12/10	2	1	4.	Look Away	Chicago
538	3/12	2	1	5.	Never Gonna Give You Up	Rick Astley
539	9/10	2	1	6.	Sweet Child O' Mine	Guns N' Roses
540	5/14	2	1	7.	Anything For You	Gloria Estefan
544	4/9	2	1	8.	Get Outta My Dreams, Get Into My Car	Billy Ocean
552	3/26	2	1	9.	Man In The Mirror	Michael Jackson
583	7/9	2	1	10.	The Flame	Cheap Trick
590	2/6	2	1	11.	Could've Been	Tiffany
596	9/24	2	1	12.	Don't Worry Be Happy	Bobby McFerrin
597	10/22	2	1	13.	Groovy Kind Of Love	Phil Collins
603	4/23	2	1	14.	Where Do Broken Hearts Go	Whitney Houston
605	2/27	2	1	15.	Father Figure	George Michael
607	11/19	2	1	16.	Bad Medicine	Bon Jovi
615	8/27	2	1	17.	Monkey	George Michael
731	1/30	1	1	18.	Need You Tonight	INXS
741	1/16	1	1	19.	Got My Mind Set On You	George Harrison
758	1/9	1	1	20.	So Emotional	Whitney Houston
777	11/12	1	1	21.	Wild, Wild West	The Escape Club
868	2/20	1	1	22.	Seasons Change	Exposé
869	5/7	1	1	23.	Wishing Well	Terence Trent D'Arby
870	12/3	1	1	24.	Baby, I Love Your Way/Freebird Medley (Free Baby)	Will To Power
882	7/23	1	1	25.	Hold On To The Nights	Richard Marx
886	6/25	1	1	26.	Foolish Beat	Debbie Gibson
894	10/8	1	1	27.	Love Bites	Def Leppard
902	1/23	1	1	28.	The Way You Make Me Feel	Michael Jackson
911	10/15	1	1	29.	Red Red Wine	UB40
916	6/18	1	1	30.	Together Forever	Rick Astley
940	11/5	1	1	31.	Kokomo	The Beach Boys
956	7/2	1	1	32.	Dirty Diana	Michael Jackson
	5/14	3	2	33.	Shattered Dreams	Johnny Hates Jazz
	8/6	2	2	34.	Hands To Heaven	Breathe
	3/26	2	2	35.	Endless Summer Nights	Richard Marx
	9/10	2	2	36.	Simply Irresistible	Robert Palmer
	2/20	2	2	37.	What Have I Done To Deserve This?	Pet Shop Boys/Dusty Springfield
	4/16	2	2	38.	Devil Inside	INXS
	7/9	2	2	39.	Mercedes Boy	Pebbles
	7/23	1	2	40.	Pour Some Sugar On Me	Def Leppard

RANK	PEAK DATE	PEAK WKS	PEAK POS		TITLE	ARTIST
202	12/23	4	1	1.	Another Day In Paradise	Phil Collins
233	10/7	4	1	2.	Miss You Much	Janet Jackson
348	2/11	3	1	3.	Straight Up	Paula Abdul
357	8/12	3	1	4.	Right Here Waiting	Richard Marx
362	3/4	3	1	5.	Lost In Your Eyes	Debbie Gibson
363	4/22	3	1	6.	Like A Prayer	Madonna
496	12/9	2	1	7.	We Didn't Start The Fire	Billy Joel
550	1/21	2	1	8.	Two Hearts	Phil Collins
580	11/11	2	1	9.	When I See You Smile	Bad English
584	11/25	2	1	10.	Blame It On The Rain	Milli Vanilli
585	5/20	2	1	11.	Forever Your Girl	Paula Abdul
586	9/23	2	1	12.	Girl I'm Gonna Miss You	Milli Vanilli
599	7/22	2	1	13.	Toy Soldiers	Martika
742	9/2	1	1	14.	Cold Hearted	Paula Abdul
762	9/16	1	1	15.	Don't Wanna Lose You	Gloria Estefan
780	6/10	1	1	16.	Wind Beneath My Wings	Bette Midler
783	1/14	1	1	17.	My Prerogative	Bobby Brown
795	4/15	1	1	18.	She Drives Me Crazy	Fine Young Cannibals
820	4/8	1	1	19.	The Look	Roxette
871	7/15	1	1	20.	If You Don't Know Me By Now	Simply Red
880	11/4	1	1	21.	Listen To Your Heart	Roxette
881	6/17	1	1	22.	I'll Be Loving You (Forever)	New Kids On The Block
883	7/1	1	1	23.	Baby Don't Forget My Number	Milli Vanilli
885	3/25	1	1	24.	The Living Years	Mike & The Mechanics
890	4/1	1	1	25.	Eternal Flame	Bangles
895	5/13	1	1	26.	I'll Be There For You	Bon Jovi
905	7/8	1	1	27.	Good Thing	Fine Young Cannibals
920	9/9	1	1	28.	Hangin' Tough	New Kids On The Block
927	8/5	1	1	29.	Batdance	Prince
945	2/4	1	1	30.	When I'm With You	Sheriff
946	6/3	1	1	31.	Rock On	Michael Damian
951	6/24	1	1	32.	Satisfied	Richard Marx
	8/5	3	2	33.	On Our Own	Bobby Brown
	12/23	2	2	34.	Don't Know Much	Linda Ronstadt feat. Aaron Neville
	9/23	2	2	35.	Heaven	Warrant
	5/20	2	2	36.	Real Love	Jody Watley
	10/7	2	2	37.	Cherish	Madonna
	7/15	2	2	38.	Express Yourself	Madonna
	4/1	1	2	39.	Girl You Know It's True	Milli Vanilli
	1/21	1	2	40.	Don't Rush Me	Taylor Dayne

TOP 40 HITS   1990

RANK	PEAK DATE	PEAK WKS	PEAK POS		TITLE	ARTIST
197	12/8	4	1	1.	Because I Love You (The Postman Song)	Stevie B
199	4/21	4	1	2.	Nothing Compares 2 U	Sinéad O'Connor
240	8/4	4	1	3.	Vision Of Love	Mariah Carey
314	5/19	3	1	4.	Vogue	Madonna
321	3/3	3	1	5.	Escapade	Janet Jackson
347	11/10	3	1	6.	Love Takes Time	Mariah Carey
352	2/10	3	1	7.	Opposites Attract	Paula Abdul (with The Wild Pair)
369	6/30	3	1	8.	Step By Step	New Kids On The Block
377	1/20	3	1	9.	How Am I Supposed To Live Without You	Michael Bolton
444	6/16	2	1	10.	It Must Have Been Love	Roxette
533	3/24	2	1	11.	Black Velvet	Alannah Myles
535	9/15	2	1	12.	Release Me	Wilson Phillips
546	7/21	2	1	13.	She Ain't Worth It	Glenn Medeiros/Bobby Brown
692	6/9	1	1	14.	Hold On	Wilson Phillips
754	9/8	1	1	15.	Blaze Of Glory	Jon Bon Jovi
757	12/1	1	1	16.	I'm Your Baby Tonight	Whitney Houston
775	10/6	1	1	17.	Close To You	Maxi Priest
782	10/20	1	1	18.	I Don't Have The Heart	James Ingram
787	11/3	1	1	19.	Ice Ice Baby	Vanilla Ice
794	9/29	1	1	20.	(Can't Live Without Your) Love And Affection	Nelson
817	9/1	1	1	21.	If Wishes Came True	Sweet Sensation
875	4/7	1	1	22.	Love Will Lead You Back	Taylor Dayne
934	10/13	1	1	23.	Praying For Time	George Michael
949	4/14	1	1	24.	I'll Be Your Everything	Tommy Page
955	10/27	1	1	25.	Black Cat	Janet Jackson
	4/14	3	2	26.	Don't Wanna Fall In Love	Jane Child
	1/20	2	2	27.	Pump Up The Jam	Technotronic f/ Felly
	5/26	2	2	28.	All I Wanna Do Is Make Love To You	Heart
	2/10	2	2	29.	Two To Make It Right	Seduction
	1/6	2	2	30.	Rhythm Nation	Janet Jackson
	3/3	2	2	31.	Dangerous	Roxette
	8/18	2	2	32.	Come Back To Me	Janet Jackson
	11/10	2	2	33.	Pray	M.C. Hammer
	12/15	1	2	34.	From A Distance	Bette Midler
	8/4	1	2	35.	Cradle Of Love	Billy Idol
	7/21	1	2	36.	Hold On	En Vogue
	8/11	1	2	37.	The Power	Snap!
	5/5	1	2	38.	I Wanna Be Rich	Calloway
	11/24	1	2	39.	More Than Words Can Say	Alias
	6/9	4	3	40.	Poison	Bell Biv DeVoe

TOP 40 HITS   1991

RANK	PEAK DATE	PEAK WKS	PEAK POS		TITLE	ARTIST
69	7/27	7	1	1.	(Everything I Do) I Do It For You	Bryan Adams
70	12/7	7	1	2.	Black Or White	Michael Jackson
143	6/15	5	1	3.	Rush, Rush	Paula Abdul
346	10/12	3	1	4.	Emotions	Mariah Carey
443	2/9	2	1	5.	Gonna Make You Sweat (Everybody Dance Now)	C & C Music Factory
483	1/26	2	1	6.	The First Time	Surface
506	5/25	2	1	7.	I Don't Wanna Cry	Mariah Carey
510	1/5	2	1	8.	Justify My Love	Madonna
529	4/27	2	1	9.	Baby Baby	Amy Grant
530	11/9	2	1	10.	Cream	Prince & The N.P.G.
534	2/23	2	1	11.	All The Man That I Need	Whitney Houston
537	3/9	2	1	12.	Someday	Mariah Carey
542	9/21	2	1	13.	I Adore Mi Amor	Color Me Badd
545	3/30	2	1	14.	Coming Out Of The Dark	Gloria Estefan
695	6/8	1	1	15.	More Than Words	Extreme
696	5/18	1	1	16.	I Like The Way (The Kissing Game)	Hi-Five
697	3/23	1	1	17.	One More Try	Timmy -T-
700	7/20	1	1	18.	Unbelievable	EMF
703	11/23	1	1	19.	When A Man Loves A Woman	Michael Bolton
729	11/30	1	1	20.	Set Adrift On Memory Bliss	PM Dawn
774	11/2	1	1	21.	Romantic	Karyn White
785	1/19	1	1	22.	Love Will Never Do (Without You)	Janet Jackson
789	10/5	1	1	23.	Good Vibrations	Marky Mark & Funky Bunch
806	4/20	1	1	24.	You're In Love	Wilson Phillips
887	5/11	1	1	25.	Joyride	Roxette
888	4/13	1	1	26.	I've Been Thinking About You	Londonbeat
950	9/14	1	1	27.	The Promise Of A New Day	Paula Abdul
	12/14	4	2	28.	It's So Hard To Say Goodbye To Yesterday	Boyz II Men
	6/8	4	2	29.	I Wanna Sex You Up	Color Me Badd
	10/19	2	2	30.	Do Anything	Natural Selection
	5/18	2	2	31.	Touch Me (All Night Long)	Cathy Dennis
	8/3	2	2	32.	P.A.S.S.I.O.N.	Rythm Syndicate
	7/27	1	2	33.	Right Here, Right Now	Jesus Jones
	11/16	1	2	34.	Can't Stop This Thing We Started	Bryan Adams
	8/17	1	2	35.	Every Heartbeat	Amy Grant
	8/24	1	2	36.	It Ain't Over 'Til It's Over	Lenny Kravitz
	8/31	1	2	37.	Fading Like A Flower (Every Time You Leave)	Roxette
	9/7	3	3	38.	Motownphilly	Boyz II Men
	1/12	2	3	39.	High Enough	Damn Yankees
	4/13	1	3	40.	Hold You Tight	Tara Kemp

RANK	PEAK DATE	PEAK WKS	PEAK POS		TITLE	ARTIST
6	11/28	14	1	1.	I Will Always Love You	Whitney Houston
7	8/15	13	1	2.	End of the Road	Boyz II Men
45	4/25	8	1	3.	Jump	Kris Kross
111	7/4	5	1	4.	Baby Got Back	Sir Mix-A-Lot
119	3/21	5	1	5.	Save The Best For Last	Vanessa Williams
269	2/8	3	1	6.	I'm Too Sexy	Right Said Fred
296	2/29	3	1	7.	To Be With You	Mr. Big
430	11/14	2	1	8.	How Do You Talk To An Angel	The Heights
503	6/20	2	1	9.	I'll Be There	Mariah Carey
645	1/25	1	1	10.	All 4 Love	Color Me Badd
736	2/1	1	1	11.	Don't Let The Sun Go Down On Me	George Michael/Elton John
755	8/8	1	1	12.	This Used To Be My Playground	Madonna
982	11/21	8	2	13.	If I Ever Fall In Love	Shai
992	8/15	6	2	14.	Baby-Baby-Baby	TLC
994	9/26	6	2	15.	Sometimes Love Just Ain't Enough	Patty Smyth with Don Henley
	3/28	4	2	16.	Tears In Heaven	Eric Clapton
	12/26	3	2	17.	Rump Shaker	Wreckx-N-Effect
	5/16	3	2	18.	My Lovin' (You're Never Gonna Get It)	En Vogue
	2/1	3	2	19.	I Love Your Smile	Shanice
	6/6	1	2	20.	Under The Bridge	Red Hot Chili Peppers
	1/25	1	2	21.	Can't Let Go	Mariah Carey
	5/9	1	2	22.	Bohemian Rhapsody	Queen
	10/31	4	3	23.	I'd Die Without You	PM Dawn
	3/7	4	3	24.	Remember The Time	Michael Jackson
	9/12	3	3	25.	Humpin' Around	Bobby Brown
	10/10	2	3	26.	Jump Around	House Of Pain
	8/29	2	3	27.	November Rain	Guns N' Roses
	4/11	1	3	28.	Masterpiece	Atlantic Starr
	2/15	1	3	29.	Diamonds And Pearls	Prince & The N.P.G.
	10/24	1	3	30.	Erotica	Madonna
	7/18	3	4	31.	Achy Breaky Heart	Billy Ray Cyrus
	5/23	2	4	32.	Live And Learn	Joe Public
	7/11	1	4	33.	If You Asked Me To	Celine Dion
	9/19	1	4	34.	Stay	Shakespear's Sister
	1/18	2	5	35.	Finally	Ce Ce Peniston
	6/27	2	5	36.	Damn I Wish I Was Your Lover	Sophie B. Hawkins
	8/1	1	5	37.	Just Another Day	Jon Secada
	10/17	1	5	38.	She's Playing Hard To Get	Hi-Five
	4/11	1	5	39.	Make It Happen	Mariah Carey
	1/11	1	5	40.	2 Legit 2 Quit	Hammer

TOP 40 HITS   1993

RANK	PEAK DATE	PEAK WKS	PEAK POS		TITLE	ARTIST
42	9/11	8	1	1.	Dreamlover	Mariah Carey
43	5/15	8	1	2.	That's The Way Love Goes	Janet Jackson
54	7/24	7	1	3.	Can't Help Falling In Love	UB40
59	3/13	7	1	4.	Informer	Snow
117	11/6	5	1	5.	I'd Do Anything For Love (But I Won't Do That)	Meat Loaf
163	12/25	4	1	6.	Hero	Mariah Carey
389	5/1	2	1	7.	Freak Me	Silk
392	7/10	2	1	8.	Weak	SWV
393	12/11	2	1	9.	Again	Janet Jackson
674	3/6	1	1	10.	A Whole New World (Aladdin's Theme)	Peabo Bryson & Regina Belle
985	7/31	7	2	11.	Whoomp! (There It Is)	Tag Team
	11/6	3	2	12.	All That She Wants	Ace Of Base
	10/2	3	2	13.	Right Here/Human Nature	SWV
	3/20	1	2	14.	Nuthin' But A "G" Thang	Dr. Dre
	10/23	1	2	15.	Just Kickin' It	Xscape
	5/22	7	3	16.	Knockin' Da Boots	H-Town
	1/16	3	3	17.	In The Still Of The Nite (I'll Remember)	Boyz II Men
	2/20	3	3	18.	Ordinary World	Duran Duran
	10/16	1	3	19.	The River Of Dreams	Billy Joel
	5/15	1	3	20.	Love Is	Vanessa Williams & Brian McKnight
	8/21	1	3	21.	I'm Gonna Be (500 Miles)	The Proclaimers
	4/3	5	4	22.	I Have Nothing	Whitney Houston
	9/11	2	4	23.	If	Janet Jackson
	11/20	2	4	24.	Gangsta Lean	D.R.S.
	1/30	2	4	25.	Saving Forever For You	Shanice
	8/28	2	4	26.	Lately	Jodeci
	2/20	2	4	27.	I'm Every Woman	Whitney Houston
	3/27	1	4	28.	Don't Walk Away	Jade
	12/4	1	4	29.	Shoop	Salt-N-Pepa
	8/21	1	4	30.	Slam	Onyx
	8/28	3	5	31.	Runaway Train	Soul Asylum
	6/19	3	5	32.	Have I Told You Lately	Rod Stewart
	1/2	1	5	33.	Rhythm Is A Dancer	Snap!
	6/12	1	5	34.	Show Me Love	Robin S
	5/22	2	6	35.	I'm So Into You	SWV
	2/20	2	6	36.	Mr. Wendal	Arrested Development
	5/29	2	6	37.	Looking Through Patient Eyes	PM Dawn
	10/30	2	6	38.	Hey Mr. D.J.	Zhané
	4/10	1	6	39.	Cats In The Cradle	Ugly Kid Joe
	8/7	3	7	40.	If I Had No Loot	Tony Toni Tone

TOP 40 HITS — 1994

RANK	PEAK DATE	PEAK WKS	PEAK POS		TITLE	ARTIST
4	8/27	14	1	1.	I'll Make Love To You	Boyz II Men
14	5/21	11	1	2.	I Swear	All-4-One
71	3/12	6	1	3.	The Sign	Ace Of Base
77	12/3	6	1	4.	On Bended Knee	Boyz II Men
161	2/12	4	1	5.	The Power Of Love	Celine Dion
178	4/9	4	1	6.	Bump N' Grind	R. Kelly
253	8/6	3	1	7.	Stay (I Missed You)	Lisa Loeb & Nine Stories
257	1/22	3	1	8.	All For Love	Bryan Adams/Rod Stewart/Sting
391	12/17	2	1	9.	Here Comes The Hotstepper	Ini Kamoze
991	10/8	6	2	10.	All I Wanna Do	Sheryl Crow
	5/28	4	2	11.	I'll Remember	Madonna
	7/2	3	2	12.	Regulate	Warren G. & Nate Dogg
	6/25	1	2	13.	Any Time, Any Place	Janet Jackson
	10/1	1	2	14.	Endless Love	Luther Vandross & Mariah Carey
	11/12	11	3	15.	Another Night	Real McCoy
	3/19	6	3	16.	Without You	Mariah Carey
	7/30	5	3	17.	Fantastic Voyage	Coolio
	1/22	3	3	18.	Breathe Again	Toni Braxton
	2/26	3	3	19.	Whatta Man	Salt 'N' Pepa with En Vogue
	4/30	3	3	20.	The Most Beautiful Girl In The World	Prince
	9/3	2	3	21.	Wild Night	John Mellencamp/Me'Shell Ndegéocello
	11/5	1	3	22.	Secret	Madonna
	9/17	1	3	23.	Stroke You Up	Changing Faces
	12/10	6	4	24.	Always	Bon Jovi
	9/10	5	4	25.	When Can I See You	Babyface
	6/18	4	4	26.	Don't Turn Around	Ace Of Base
	4/16	2	4	27.	Mmm Mmm Mmm Mmm	Crash Test Dummies
	5/7	2	4	28.	Return To Innocence	Enigma
	8/6	1	4	29.	Can You Feel The Love Tonight	Elton John
	3/12	3	5	30.	So Much In Love	All-4-One
	7/2	1	5	31.	Back & Forth	Aaliyah
	10/15	1	5	32.	Never Lie	Immature
	5/14	4	6	33.	Baby, I Love Your Way	Big Mountain
	12/31	3	6	34.	I Wanna Be Down	Brandy
	1/22	2	6	35.	Said I Loved You...But I Lied	Michael Bolton
	10/15	2	6	36.	At Your Best (You Are Love)	Aaliyah
	8/13	1	6	37.	Funkdafied	Da Brat
	5/28	4	7	38.	You Mean The World To Me	Toni Braxton
	3/19	3	7	39.	Now and Forever	Richard Marx
	2/12	1	7	40.	Getto Jam	Domino

RANK	PEAK DATE	PEAK WKS	PEAK POS		TITLE	ARTIST
1	12/2	16	1	1.	One Sweet Day	Mariah Carey & Boyz II Men
38	9/30	8	1	2.	Fantasy	Mariah Carey
49	7/8	7	1	3.	Waterfalls	TLC
53	2/25	7	1	4.	Take A Bow	Madonna
56	4/15	7	1	5.	This Is How We Do It	Montell Jordan
120	6/3	5	1	6.	Have You Ever Really Loved A Woman?	Bryan Adams
154	1/28	4	1	7.	Creep	TLC
247	9/9	3	1	8.	Gangsta's Paradise	Coolio f/ L.V.
639	8/26	1	1	9.	Kiss From A Rose	Seal
642	11/25	1	1	10.	Exhale (Shoop Shoop)	Whitney Houston
682	9/2	1	1	11.	You Are Not Alone	Michael Jackson
	3/18	4	2	12.	Candy Rain	Soul For Real
	7/1	3	2	13.	Don't Take It Personal (just one of dem days)	Monica
	4/15	3	2	14.	Red Light Special	TLC
	7/15	3	2	15.	One More Chance/Stay With Me	The Notorious B.I.G.
	5/6	2	2	16.	Freak Like Me	Adina Howard
	6/17	1	2	17.	Water Runs Dry	Boyz II Men
	6/24	1	2	18.	Total Eclipse Of The Heart	Nicki French
	12/2	8	3	19.	Hey Lover	LL Cool J
	10/21	5	3	20.	Runaway	Janet Jackson
	8/19	2	3	21.	Boombastic	Shaggy
	4/8	1	3	22.	Run Away	Real McCoy
	6/3	1	3	23.	I'll Be There For You/You're All I Need To Get By	Method Man f/ Mary J. Blige
	5/6	2	4	24.	I Know	Dionne Farris
	3/11	2	4	25.	Baby	Brandy
	11/18	2	4	26.	You Remind Me Of Something	R. Kelly
	8/26	1	4	27.	Colors Of The Wind	Vanessa Williams
	3/25	3	5	28.	Strong Enough	Sheryl Crow
	12/30	3	5	29.	Diggin' On You	TLC
	11/4	3	5	30.	Tell Me	Groove Theory
	6/17	2	5	31.	Scream	Michael Jackson & Janet Jackson
	8/26	1	5	32.	I Can Love You Like That	All-4-One
	3/11	1	5	33.	You Gotta Be	Des'ree
	10/28	3	6	34.	As I Lay Me Down	Sophie B. Hawkins
	3/18	2	6	35.	Big Poppa	The Notorious B.I.G.
	10/21	1	6	36.	Only Wanna Be With You	Hootie & The Blowfish
	12/16	1	6	37.	You'll See	Madonna
	1/7	4	7	38.	Before I Let You Go	BLACKstreet
	11/11	2	7	39.	Back For Good	Take That
	12/30	1	7	40.	Before You Walk Out Of My Life	Monica

TOP 40 HITS   1996

RANK	PEAK DATE	PEAK WKS	PEAK POS	TITLE	ARTIST
2	8/3	14	1	1. Macarena (bayside boys mix)	Los Del Rio
12	12/7	11	1	2. Un-Break My Heart	Toni Braxton
47	5/18	8	1	3. Tha Crossroads	Bone thugs-n-harmony
74	3/23	6	1	4. Because You Loved Me	Celine Dion
156	11/9	4	1	5. No Diggity	BLACKstreet
390	5/4	2	1	6. Always Be My Baby	Mariah Carey
424	7/13	2	1	7. How Do U Want It	2 Pac f/ KC & JoJo
636	7/27	1	1	8. You're Makin' Me High	Toni Braxton
979	8/24	9	2	9. I Love You Always Forever	Donna Lewis
999	10/26	5	2	10. It's All Coming Back To Me Now	Celine Dion
	12/21	4	2	11. I Believe I Can Fly	R. Kelly
	3/23	2	2	12. Nobody Knows	The Tony Rich Project
	3/9	2	2	13. Sittin' Up In My Room	Brandy f/ LL Cool J
	2/24	2	2	14. Not Gon' Cry	Mary J. Blige
	8/17	1	2	15. Twisted	Keith Sweat
	2/17	1	2	16. Missing	Everything But The Girl
	6/15	5	3	17. Give Me One Reason	Tracy Chapman
	12/7	2	3	18. Nobody	Keith Sweat
	8/17	1	3	19. C'Mon N' Ride It (The Train)	Quad City DJ's
	8/24	1	3	20. Loungin	LL Cool J
	8/31	1	3	21. Hit Me Off	New Edition
	4/13	5	4	22. Ironic	Alanis Morissette
	11/23	2	4	23. Mouth	Merril Bainbridge
	3/30	2	4	24. Down Low (Nobody Has To Know)	R. Kelly f/ Ronald Isley & Ernie Isley
	2/3	2	4	25. One Of Us	Joan Osborne
	10/12	3	5	26. Where Do You Go	No Mercy
	8/17	2	5	27. Change The World	Eric Clapton
	4/27	2	5	28. 1,2,3,4 (Sumpin' New)	Coolio
	1/27	1	5	29. Name	Goo Goo Dolls
	8/3	1	5	30. I Can't Sleep Baby (If I)	R. Kelly
	6/8	1	5	31. You're The One	SWV
	1/20	1	5	32. Breakfast At Tiffany's	Deep Blue Something
	2/24	3	6	33. Be My Lover	La Bouche
	11/23	2	6	34. Pony	Ginuwine
	6/22	1	6	35. California Love	2 Pac f/ Dr. Dre & Roger Troutman
	7/27	1	6	36. You Learn	Alanis Morissette
	11/9	1	6	37. This Is For The Lover In You	Babyface
	1/6	1	6	38. Free As A Bird	The Beatles
	6/22	2	7	39. Theme From Mission: Impossible	Adam Clayton & Larry Mullen
	2/24	2	7	40. Jesus To A Child	George Michael

AIRPLAY-ONLY TOP HITS:

	PEAK DATE	PEAK WKS	PEAK POS	TITLE	ARTIST
	12/7	16	1	Don't Speak	No Doubt

163

TOP 40 HITS   1997

RANK	PEAK DATE	PEAK WKS	PEAK POS	TITLE	ARTIST
5	10/11	14	1	1. Candle In The Wind 1997 / Something About The Way You Look Tonight ..... *Elton John*	
15	6/14	11	1	2. I'll Be Missing You .... *Puff Daddy & Faith Evans f/ 112*	
79	3/22	6	1	3. Can't Nobody Hold Me Down .... *Puff Daddy f/ Mase*	
167	2/22	4	1	4. Wannabe .... *Spice Girls*	
265	5/24	3	1	5. MMMBop ....*Hanson*	
312	9/13	3	1	6. Honey.. *Mariah Carey*	
319	5/3	3	1	7. Hypnotize .... *The Notorious B.I.G.*	
406	8/30	2	1	8. Mo Money Mo Problems .... *The Notorious B.I.G. f/ Puff Daddy & Mase*	
672	10/4	1	1	9. 4 Seasons Of Loneliness.. *Boyz II Men*	
986	10/25	7	2	10. You Make Me Wanna... .... *Usher*	
	12/13	4	2	11. How Do I Live .... *LeAnn Rimes*	
	1/18	4	2	12. Don't Let Go (Love) .... *En Vogue*	
	7/12	4	2	13. Bitch...*Meredith Brooks*	
	4/19	2	2	14. You Were Meant For Me..*Jewel*	
	9/6	2	2	15. Quit Playing Games (With My Heart)............... *Backstreet Boys*	
	6/7	1	2	16. Return Of The Mack .... *Mark Morrison*	
	5/31	3	3	17. Say You'll Be There................................*Spice Girls*	
	8/9	4	4	18. Semi-Charmed Life.. *Third Eye Blind*	
	4/19	4	4	19. For You I Will.. *Monica*	
	12/6	3	4	20. My Body ....*LSG*	
	4/5	2	4	21. All By Myself .... *Celine Dion*	
	11/29	1	4	22. My Love Is The Shhh! .... *Somethin' For The People*	
	3/29	1	4	23. In My Bed .... *Dru Hill*	
	9/6	1	4	24. 2 Become 1 ....*Spice Girls*	
	2/1	1	4	25. I Believe In You And Me................................ *Whitney Houston*	
	5/10	1	4	26. I Want You..*Savage Garden*	
	11/22	1	4	27. All Cried Out ....*Allure*	
	6/21	1	4	28. Look Into My Eyes................................*Bone Thugs-N-Harmony*	
	12/13	2	5	29. Feel So Good .... *Mase*	
	6/7	1	5	30. The Freshmen.. *The Verve Pipe*	
	11/29	3	6	31. Tubthumping ....*Chumbawamba*	
	3/22	3	6	32. Every Time I Close My Eyes .... *Babyface*	
	6/7	2	6	33. I Belong To You (Every Time I See Your Face) .... *Rome*	
	8/9	1	6	34. Not Tonight .... *Lil' Kim*	
	11/29	3	7	35. Show Me Love ....*Robyn*	
	11/1	2	7	36. Foolish Games...*Jewel*	
	8/2	2	7	37. Do You Know (What It Takes) ....*Robyn*	
	1/11	1	7	38. I'm Still In Love With You .... *New Edition*	
	7/26	1	7	39. Sunny Came Home... *Shawn Colvin*	
	7/19	1	7	40. It's Your Love...................................... *Tim McGraw & Faith Hill*	

AIRPLAY-ONLY TOP HITS:

	10/18	6	1	Fly .... *Sugar Ray*	
	8/9	4	1	Men In Black .... *Will Smith*	
	3/1	8	2	Lovefool.. *The Cardigans*	
	5/10	5	2	One Headlight .... *The Wallflowers*	

TOP 40 HITS   1998

RANK	PEAK DATE	PEAK WKS	PEAK POS		TITLE	ARTIST
8	6/6	13	1	1.	The Boy Is Mine	Brandy & Monica
102	12/5	6	1	2.	I'm Your Angel	R. Kelly & Celine Dion
107	4/25	5	1	3.	Too Close	Next
110	10/3	5	1	4.	The First Night	Monica
201	9/5	4	1	5.	I Don't Want To Miss A Thing	Aerosmith
262	4/4	3	1	6.	All My Life	K-Ci & JoJo
376	3/14	3	1	7.	Gettin' Jiggy Wit It	Will Smith
385	1/17	2	1	8.	Truly Madly Deeply	Savage Garden
395	1/31	2	1	9.	Together Again	Janet
397	2/14	2	1	10.	Nice & Slow	Usher
414	11/14	2	1	11.	Doo Wop (That Thing)	Lauryn Hill
488	2/28	2	1	12.	My Heart Will Go On (Love Theme From 'Titanic')	Celine Dion
646	11/28	1	1	13.	Lately	Divine
660	5/23	1	1	14.	My All	Mariah Carey
704	10/17	1	1	15.	One Week	Barenaked Ladies
978	5/2	9	2	16.	You're Still The One	Shania Twain
980	12/5	8	2	17.	Nobody's Supposed To Be Here	Deborah Cox
	8/15	3	2	18.	My Way	Usher
	4/11	2	2	19.	Let's Ride	Montell Jordan
	1/3	2	2	20.	It's All About The Benjamins	Puff Daddy
	4/4	1	2	21.	Frozen	Madonna
	9/5	4	3	22.	Crush	Jennifer Paige
	10/24	3	3	23.	How Deep Is Your Love	Dru Hill
	11/21	1	3	24.	Because Of You	98°
	8/22	1	3	25.	Adia	Sarah McLachlan
	3/28	1	3	26.	No, No, No (Part 2)	Destiny's Child
	5/23	1	3	27.	I Get Lonely	Janet Jackson
	5/9	2	4	28.	Everybody (Backstreet's Back)	Backstreet Boys
	12/19	2	4	29.	From This Moment On	Shania Twain
	7/25	1	4	30.	Come With Me	Puff Daddy
	8/22	1	4	31.	Never Ever	All Saints
	1/24	1	4	32.	Been Around The World	Puff Daddy
	8/1	3	5	33.	Make It Hot	Nicole
	10/3	2	5	34.	I'll Be	Edwin McCain
	5/16	1	5	35.	Body Bumpin' (Yippie Yi-Yo)	Public Announcement
	7/11	1	5	36.	Ray Of Light	Madonna
	2/7	3	6	37.	I Don't Ever Want To See You Again	Uncle Sam
	5/16	3	6	38.	It's All About Me	Mya
	9/12	2	6	39.	Daydreamin'	Tatyana Ali
	4/18	2	6	40.	Romeo And Juliet	Sylk-E. Fyne

AIRPLAY-ONLY TOP HITS:

	8/1	18	1	Iris	Goo Goo Dolls
	5/16	11	1	Torn	Natalie Imbruglia

RANK	PEAK DATE	PEAK WKS	PEAK POS		TITLE	ARTIST
9	10/23	12	1	1.	Smooth	Santana f/. Rob Thomas
112	6/12	5	1	2.	If You Had My Love	Jennifer Lopez
114	7/31	5	1	3.	Genie In A Bottle	Christina Aguilera
118	5/8	5	1	4.	Livin' La Vida Loca	Ricky Martin
159	4/10	4	1	5.	No Scrubs	TLC
162	3/13	4	1	6.	Believe	Cher
166	2/13	4	1	7.	Angel Of Mine	Monica
256	9/18	3	1	8.	Unpretty	TLC
396	1/30	2	1	9.	Baby One More Time	Britney Spears
402	1/16	2	1	10.	Have You Ever?	Brandy
501	10/9	2	1	11.	Heartbreaker	Mariah Carey f/ Jay-Z
579	9/4	2	1	12.	Bailamos	Enrique Iglesias
678	7/17	1	1	13.	Bills, Bills, Bills	Destiny's Child
892	7/24	1	1	14.	Wild Wild West	Will Smith f/ Dru Hill & Kool Mo Dee
981	11/20	8	2	15.	Back At One	Brian McKnight
	3/20	3	2	16.	Heartbreak Hotel	Whitney Houston f/ Faith Evans & Kelly Price
	10/30	3	2	17.	Satisfy You	Puff Daddy
	9/25	2	2	18.	She's All I Ever Had	Ricky Martin
	5/1	1	2	19.	Kiss Me	Sixpence None The Richer
	6/26	1	2	20.	Last Kiss	Pearl Jam
	8/14	1	2	21.	Tell Me It's Real	K-Ci & JoJo
	10/16	1	2	22.	Music Of My Heart	*NSYNC & Gloria Estefan
	12/11	5	3	23.	I Wanna Love You Forever	Jessica Simpson
	8/28	4	3	24.	Summer Girls	LFO
	4/3	3	3	25.	Every Morning	Sugar Ray
	11/27	2	3	26.	I Need To Know	Marc Anthony
	11/13	2	3	27.	Mambo No. 5 (A Little Bit Of.)	Lou Bega
	4/17	1	3	28.	What's It Gonna Be?!	Busta Rhymes
	5/29	3	4	29.	Fortunate	Maxwell
	3/6	2	4	30.	Angel	Sarah McLachlan
	3/20	2	4	31.	I Still Believe	Mariah Carey
	6/19	1	4	32.	Where My Girls At?	702
	8/14	1	4	33.	All Star	Smash Mouth
	7/3	1	4	34.	It's Not Right But It's Okay	Whitney Houston
	2/6	2	5	35.	All I Have To Give	Backstreet Boys
	5/22	1	5	36.	Who Dat	JT Money
	1/23	1	5	37.	Save Tonight	Eagle-Eye Cherry
	7/3	1	5	38.	The Hardest Thing	98°
	1/30	1	5	39.	Jumper	Third Eye Blind
	9/11	1	5	40.	Lost In You	Garth Brooks as Chris Gaines

RANK	PEAK DATE	PEAK WKS	PEAK POS		TITLE	ARTIST
16	11/18	11	1	1.	Independent Women Part I	Destiny's Child
18	4/8	10	1	2.	Maria Maria	Santana f/ The Product G&B
158	1/29	4	1	3.	I Knew I Loved You	Savage Garden
179	9/16	4	1	4.	Music	Madonna
229	10/14	4	1	5.	Come On Over Baby (all I want is you)	Christina Aguilera
264	8/26	3	1	6.	Doesn't Really Matter	Janet Jackson
270	3/18	3	1	7.	Say My Name	Destiny's Child
283	6/24	3	1	8.	Be With You	Enrique Iglesias
403	8/12	2	1	9.	Incomplete	Sisqó
405	3/4	2	1	10.	Amazed	Lonestar
412	7/29	2	1	11.	It's Gonna Be Me	*NSYNC
528	1/15	2	1	12.	What A Girl Wants	Christina Aguilera
637	7/15	1	1	13.	Everything You Want	Vertical Horizon
638	11/11	1	1	14.	With Arms Wide Open	Creed
641	6/17	1	1	15.	Try Again	Aaliyah
644	7/22	1	1	16.	Bent	Matchbox Twenty
970	2/19	1	1	17.	Thank God I Found You	Mariah with Joe & 98°
998	4/22	5	2	18.	Breathe	Faith Hill
	12/2	3	2	19.	Case Of The Ex (Whatcha Gonna Do)	Mya
	12/30	2	2	20.	He Loves U Not	Dream
	5/6	2	2	21.	He Wasn't Man Enough	Toni Braxton
	6/3	2	2	22.	You Sang To Me	Marc Anthony
	9/30	2	2	23.	Give Me Just One Night (Una Noche)	98°
	8/19	5	3	24.	Jumpin', Jumpin'	Destiny's Child
	11/11	3	3	25.	Kryptonite	3 Doors Down
	5/20	3	3	26.	Thong Song	Sisqó
	7/1	2	3	27.	I Turn To You	Christina Aguilera
	1/1	2	4	28.	My Love Is Your Love	Whitney Houston
	7/1	2	4	29.	I Wanna Know	Joe
	2/12	2	4	30.	Get It On...Tonite	Montell Jordan
	4/15	2	4	31.	Bye Bye Bye	*NSYNC
	6/24	2	4	32.	The Real Slim Shady	Eminem
	11/25	1	4	33.	Most Girls	Pink
	12/9	1	4	34.	Gotta Tell You	Samantha Mumba
	1/22	2	5	35.	Bring It All To Me	Blaque f/ *NSYNC
	1/8	1	5	36.	Hot Boyz	Missy "Misdemeanor" Elliott f/ Nas, Eve & Q-Tip
	5/20	1	5	37.	I Try	Macy Gray
	12/2	1	5	38.	This I Promise You	*NSYNC
	9/2	1	5	39.	No More	Ruff Endz
	3/18	3	6	40.	Show Me The Meaning Of Being Lonely	Backstreet Boys

RANK	PEAK DATE	PEAK WKS	PEAK POS		TITLE	ARTIST
57	4/14	7	1	1.	All For You	Janet Jackson
72	12/15	6	1	2.	U Got It Bad	Usher
73	11/3	6	1	3.	Family Affair	Mary J. Blige
75	8/18	6	1	4.	Fallin'	Alicia Keys
108	9/8	5	1	5.	I'm Real	Jennifer Lopez f/ Ja Rule
122	6/2	5	1	6.	Lady Marmalade	Christina Aguilera, Lil' Kim, Mya & P!nk
153	12/22	4	1	7.	How You Remind Me	Nickelback
165	7/7	4	1	8.	U Remind Me	Usher
168	2/24	4	1	9.	Stutter	Joe f/ Mystikal
388	2/3	2	1	10.	It Wasn't Me	Shaggy f/ Ricardo "RikRok" Ducent
484	3/24	2	1	11.	Butterfly	Crazy Town
609	8/4	2	1	12.	Bootylicious	Destiny's Child
647	3/31	1	1	13.	Angel	Shaggy f/ Rayvon
657	2/17	1	1	14.	Ms. Jackson	OutKast
989	4/14	7	2	15.	Survivor	Destiny's Child
	6/16	4	2	16.	Hanging By A Moment	Lifehouse
	7/21	2	2	17.	Hit 'Em Up Style (Oops!)	Blu Cantrell
	8/4	2	2	18.	Loverboy	Mariah Carey
	8/18	1	2	19.	Let Me Blow Ya Mind	Eve f/ Gwen Stefani
	9/15	5	3	20.	Where The Party At	Jagged Edge f/ Nelly
	11/17	3	3	21.	Hero	Enrique Iglesias
	4/28	3	3	22.	Thankyou	Dido
	2/24	2	3	23.	Love Don't Cost A Thing	Jennifer Lopez
	9/1	2	3	24.	Someone To Call My Lover	Janet Jackson
	6/23	1	3	25.	Ride Wit Me	Nelly f/ City Spud
	7/28	1	3	26.	All Or Nothing	O-Town
	6/30	1	3	27.	My Baby	Lil' Romeo
	2/17	6	4	28.	Again	Lenny Kravitz
	12/29	6	4	29.	Get The Party Started	P!nk
	10/27	2	4	30.	Differences	Ginuwine
	7/7	2	4	31.	Peaches & Cream	One Twelve
	2/3	2	4	32.	Don't Tell Me	Madonna
	4/28	1	4	33.	Missing You	Case
	11/10	4	5	34.	Turn Off The Light	Nelly Furtado
	6/23	2	5	35.	Drops Of Jupiter (Tell Me)	Train
	6/9	2	5	36.	Follow Me	Uncle Kracker
	10/20	1	5	37.	It's Been Awhile	Staind
	1/27	1	5	38.	If You're Gone	Matchbox Twenty
	12/29	2	6	39.	Whenever, Wherever	Shakira
	1/13	1	6	40.	The Way You Love Me	Faith Hill

TOP 40 HITS　　　　2002

RANK	PEAK DATE	PEAK WKS	PEAK POS	TITLE	ARTIST
11	11/9	12	1	1. Lose Yourself	Eminem
17	8/17	10	1	2. Dilemma	Nelly f/ Kelly Rowland
19	4/20	10	1	3. Foolish	Ashanti
50	6/29	7	1	4. Hot In Herre	Nelly
83	3/9	6	1	5. Ain't It Funny	Jennifer Lopez f/ Ja Rule
387	2/23	2	1	6. Always On Time	Ja Rule f/ Ashanti
563	10/5	2	1	7. A Moment Like This	Kelly Clarkson
976	11/16	10	2	8. Work It	Missy "Misdemeanor" Elliott
988	4/6	7	2	9. What's Luv?	Fat Joe f/ Ashanti
	6/29	5	2	10. Without Me	Eminem
	9/14	4	2	11. Gangsta Lovin'	Eve f/ Alicia Keys
	5/25	4	2	12. I Need A Girl (Part One)	P. Diddy f/ Usher & Loon
	8/3	2	2	13. Complicated	Avril Lavigne
	3/30	1	2	14. In The End	Linkin Park
	12/7	4	3	15. Jenny From The Block	Jennifer Lopez f/ Jadakiss & Styles
	11/23	2	3	16. Underneath It All	No Doubt f/ Lady Saw
	7/13	2	3	17. Hero	Chad Kroeger f/ Josey Scott
	5/4	1	3	18. U Don't Have To Call	Usher
	11/2	1	3	19. Hey Ma	Cam'ron f/ Juelz Santana, Freekey Zekey & Toya
	8/3	3	4	20. I Need A Girl (Part Two)	P. Diddy & Ginuwine f/ Loon, Mario Winans & Tammy Ruggeri)
	12/28	3	4	21. '03 Bonnie & Clyde	Jay-Z f/ Beyoncé
	11/16	3	4	22. Luv U Better	LL Cool J
	7/6	2	4	23. Oh Boy	Cam'ron f/ Juelz Santana
	8/24	2	4	24. Just A Friend 2002	Mario
	9/21	2	4	25. Cleanin' Out My Closet	Eminem
	2/9	1	4	26. My Sacrifice	Creed
	4/6	4	5	27. Girlfriend	*NSYNC f/ Nelly
	5/18	3	5	28. A Thousand Miles	Vanessa Carlton
	11/30	3	5	29. The Game Of Love	Santana f/ Michelle Branch
	3/16	2	5	30. Wherever You Will Go	The Calling
	3/2	2	5	31. Hey Baby	No Doubt f/ Bounty Killer
	5/11	1	5	32. Blurry	Puddle Of Mudd
	6/22	1	5	33. The Middle	Jimmy Eat World
	9/28	3	6	34. One Last Breath	Creed
	5/25	1	6	35. All You Wanted	Michelle Branch
	8/17	1	6	36. Down 4 U	Irv Gotte Presents The Inc. f/ Ja Rule, Ashanti, Charli Baltimore & Vita
	5/4	1	7	37. Oops (Oh My)	Tweet
	2/9	1	7	38. A Woman's Worth	Alicia Keys
	12/7	1	7	39. Gimme The Light	Sean Paul
	3/16	1	7	40. What About Us?	Brandy

TOP 40 HITS   2003

RANK	PEAK DATE	PEAK WKS	PEAK POS		TITLE	ARTIST
25	12/13	9	1	1.	Hey Ya!	OutKast
26	3/8	9	1	2.	In Da Club	50 Cent
28	10/4	9	1	3.	Baby Boy	Beyoncé f/ Sean Paul
37	7/12	8	1	4.	Crazy In Love	Beyoncé f/ Jay-Z
173	5/31	4	1	5.	21 Questions	50 Cent f/ Nate Dogg
177	9/6	4	1	6.	Shake Ya Tailfeather	Nelly/P. Diddy/Murphy Lee
181	2/8	4	1	7.	All I Have	Jennifer Lopez f/ LL Cool J
250	5/10	3	1	8.	Get Busy	Sean Paul
634	6/28	2	1	9.	This Is The Night	Clay Aiken
640	12/6	1	1	10.	Stand Up	Ludacris f/ Shawnna
664	2/1	1	1	11.	Bump, Bump, Bump	B2K & P. Diddy
1000	8/9	5	2	12.	Right Thurr	Chingy
	3/29	5	2	13.	Ignition	R. Kelly
	7/12	3	2	14.	Magic Stick	Lil' Kim f/ 50 Cent
	6/28	2	2	15.	Flying Without Wings	Ruben Studdard
	10/25	1	2	16.	Get Low	Lil Jon & The East Side Boyz f/ Ying Yang Twins
	2/1	1	2	17.	Beautiful	Christina Aguilera
	2/15	1	2	18.	Mesmerize	Ja Rule f/ Ashanti
	8/2	1	2	19.	Rock Wit U (Awww Baby)	Ashanti
	12/27	5	3	20.	Milkshake	Kelis
	1/4	4	3	21.	Air Force Ones	Nelly f/ Kyjuan, Ali & Murphy Lee
	5/31	3	3	22.	I Know What You Want	Busta Rhymes & Mariah Carey f/ The Flipmode Squad
	11/8	3	3	23.	Holidae In	Chingy f/ Ludacris & Snoop Dogg
	4/5	1	3	24.	Miss You	Aaliyah
	8/23	1	3	25.	P.I.M.P.	50 Cent
	2/1	1	3	26.	Cry Me A River	Justin Timberlake
	8/16	1	3	27.	Never Leave You – Uh Oooh, Oh Oooh!	Lumidee
	4/5	3	4	28.	Picture	Kid Rock f/ Sheryl Crow
	11/1	3	4	29.	Damn!	Youngbloodz f/ Lil' Jon
	5/31	3	4	30.	Can't Let You Go	Fabolous f/ Mike Shorey & Lil' Mo
	2/1	2	4	31.	I'm With You	Avril Lavigne
	4/26	1	4	32.	When I'm Gone	3 Doors Down
	9/20	1	4	33.	Into You	Fabolous f/ Tamia or Ashanti
	5/3	1	4	34.	God Bless The U.S.A.	American Idol Finalists
	11/8	3	5	35.	Here Without You	3 Doors Down
	9/20	3	5	36.	Frontin'	Pharrell f/ Jay-Z
	7/19	2	5	37.	Unwell	Matchbox Twenty
	6/7	1	5	38.	Bring Me To Life	Evanescence
	5/10	1	5	39.	Rock Your Body	Justin Timberlake
	12/20	5	6	40.	Walked Outta Heaven	Jagged Edge

TOP 40 HITS   2004

RANK	PEAK DATE	PEAK WKS	PEAK POS	TITLE	ARTIST
10	2/28	12	1	1. Yeah!	Usher f/ Lil' Jon & Ludacris
36	5/22	8	1	2. Burn	Usher
51	9/11	7	1	3. Goodies	Ciara f/ Petey Pablo
76	10/30	6	1	4. My Boo	Usher & Alicia Keys
249	12/11	3	1	5. Drop It Like It's Hot	Snoop Dogg f/ Pharrell
251	8/21	3	1	6. Lean Back	Terror Squad
401	7/24	2	1	7. Confessions Part II	Usher
407	8/7	2	1	8. Slow Motion	Juvenile f/ Soulja Slim
635	2/14	1	1	9. The Way You Move	OutKast f/ Sleepy Brown
652	2/21	1	1	10. Slow Jamz	Twista f/ Kanye West & Jamie Foxx
975	7/10	1	1	11. I Believe	Fantasia
983	4/24	8	2	12. I Don't Wanna Know	Mario Winans f/ P. Diddy & Enya
	3/13	5	2	13. One Call Away	Chingy f/ J. Weav
	8/28	2	2	14. Sunshine	Lil' Flip f/ Lea
	6/19	1	2	15. The Reason	Hoobastank
	4/17	1	2	16. Tipsy	J-Kwon
	10/30	4	3	17. Lose My Breath	Destiny's Child
	6/5	2	3	18. Naughty Girl	Beyoncé
	12/4	1	3	19. Over And Over	Nelly f/ Tim McGraw
	1/31	1	3	20. You Don't Know My Name	Alicia Keys
	9/4	7	4	21. My Place	Nelly f/ Jaheim
	2/21	2	4	22. Me, Myself And I	Beyoncé
	8/14	2	4	23. Turn Me On	Kevin Lyttle
	7/3	1	4	24. If I Ain't Got You	Alicia Keys
	8/7	1	4	25. Move Ya Body	Nina Sky f/ Jabba
	3/27	1	4	26. Hotel	Cassidy f/ R. Kelly
	4/3	1	4	27. Solitaire	Clay Aiken
	4/24	3	5	28. This Love	Maroon5
	9/25	3	5	29. She Will Be Loved	Maroon5
	8/21	2	5	30. Dip It Low	Christina Milian
	11/27	1	5	31. Wonderful	Ja Rule f/ R. Kelly & Ashanti
	4/10	1	5	32. Dirt Off Your Shoulder	Jay-Z
	9/18	1	5	33. Pieces Of Me	Ashlee Simpson
	5/22	5	6	34. Overnight Celebrity	Twista
	3/20	2	6	35. Splash Waterfalls	Ludacris
	10/30	2	6	36. Just Lose It	Eminem
	11/20	1	6	37. Breakaway	Kelly Clarkson
	5/15	1	6	38. My Band	D12
	11/27	2	7	39. Let's Go	Trick Daddy f/ Twista & Lil Jon
	7/3	1	7	40. Freek-A-Leek	Petey Pablo

171

TOP 40 HITS　　　　　2005

RANK	PEAK DATE	PEAK WKS	PEAK POS		TITLE	ARTIST
3	6/4	14	1	1.	We Belong Together	Mariah Carey
22	9/17	10	1	2.	Gold Digger	Kanye West f/ Jamie Foxx
24	1/1	9	1	3.	Let Me Love You	Mario
31	3/5	9	1	4.	Candy Shop	50 Cent
138	11/26	5	1	5.	Run It!	Chris Brown
155	5/7	4	1	6.	Hollaback Girl	Gwen Stefani
973	7/2	1	1	7.	Inside Your Heaven	Carrie Underwood
987	1/8	7	2	8.	1,2 Step	Ciara
993	9/10	6	2	9.	Shake It Off	Mariah Carey
	3/5	5	2	10.	Boulevard Of Broken Dreams	Green Day
	4/16	5	2	11.	Hate It Or Love It	The Game
	8/20	3	2	12.	Don't Cha	The Pussycat Dolls f/ Busta Rhymes
	7/30	3	2	13.	Pon De Replay	Rihanna
	4/9	1	2	14.	Since U Been Gone	Kelly Clarkson
	10/22	1	2	15.	Photograph	Nickelback
	5/21	1	2	16.	Oh	Ciara
	12/17	1	2	17.	Laffy Taffy	D4L
	7/9	1	2	18.	Inside Your Heaven	Bo Bice
	11/5	6	3	19.	My Humps	The Black Eyed Peas
	1/22	3	3	20.	Lovers And Friends	Lil Jon & The East Side Boyz
	6/25	3	3	21.	Don't Phunk With My Heart	Black Eyed Peas
	10/1	2	3	22.	Like You	Bow Wow f/ Ciara
	3/26	1	3	23.	Disco Inferno	50 Cent
	9/17	1	3	24.	Lose Control	Missy Elliott f/ Ciara & Fat Man Scoop
	6/18	1	3	25.	Just A Lil Bit	50 Cent
	2/12	1	3	26.	Soldier	Destiny's Child
	4/2	1	3	27.	Obsession [No Es Amor]	Frankie J
	2/19	4	4	28.	How We Do	The Game
	11/12	4	4	29.	Soul Survivor	Young Jeezy f/ Akon
	4/23	4	4	30.	Lonely	Akon
	8/13	3	4	31.	Let Me Hold You	Bob Wow f/ Omarion
	8/27	1	5	32.	You And Me	Lifehouse
	6/11	4	6	33.	Behind These Hazel Eyes	Kelly Clarkson
	11/12	3	6	34.	We Be Burnin'	Sean Paul
	10/15	2	6	35.	Wake Me Up When September Ends	Green Day
	5/21	1	6	36.	Lonely No More	Rob Thomas
	10/1	1	6	37.	Outta Control (Remix)	50 Cent f/ Mobb Deep
	12/3	2	7	38.	Hung Up	Madonna
	11/19	1	7	39.	Because Of You	Kelly Clarkson
	3/5	1	7	40.	Rich Girl	Gwen Stefani

THE ARTISTS

This section lists, alphabetically by artist name, every song listed in the Top 1000 ranking.

Each artist's hits are listed in rank order, with the Top 1000 ranking next to each title. This makes for a handy guide to quickly view each artist's all-time greatest hits.

A

AALIYAH
641 Try Again

ABBA
739 Dancing Queen

ABBOTT, Gregory
734 Shake You Down

ABDUL, Paula
143 Rush, Rush
348 Straight Up
352 Opposites Attract
     PAULA ABDUL (with The Wild Pair)
585 Forever Your Girl
742 Cold Hearted
950 The Promise Of A New Day

ACE OF BASE
71 The Sign

ADAMS, Bryan
69 (Everything I Do) I Do It For You
120 Have You Ever Really Loved A
     Woman?
257 All For Love
     BRYAN ADAMS/ROD STEWART/STING
593 Heaven

AEROSMITH
201 I Don't Want To Miss A Thing

AGUILERA, Christina
114 Genie In A Bottle
122 Lady Marmalade
     CHRISTINA AGUILERA, LIL' KIM, MYA
     and P!NK
229 Come On Over Baby (all I want is
     you)
528 What A Girl Wants

A-HA
781 Take On Me

AIKEN, Clay
634 This Is The Night

AIR SUPPLY
759 The One That You Love

ALL-4-ONE
14 I Swear

ALPERT, Herb
238 This Guy's In Love With You
452 Rise

AMERICA
295 A Horse With No Name
969 Sister Golden Hair

ANGELS, The
311 My Boyfriend's Back

ANIMALS, The
345 The House Of The Rising Sun

ANKA, Paul
204 Lonely Boy
382 (You're) Having My Baby
658 Diana

ARCHIES, The
184 Sugar, Sugar

ARMSTRONG, Louis
653 Hello, Dolly!

ASHANTI
19 Foolish
387 Always On Time
     JA RULE (feat. Ashanti)
988 What's Luv?
     FAT JOE Featuring Ashanti

ASSOCIATION, The
220 Windy
380 Cherish

ASTLEY, Rick
538 Never Gonna Give You Up
916 Together Forever

ATLANTIC STARR
797 Always

AUSTIN, Patti
438 Baby, Come To Me
     PATTI AUSTIN (with James Ingram)

AVALON, Frankie
136 Venus
724 Why

AWB (AVERAGE WHITE BAND)
826 Pick Up The Pieces

B

**BACHMAN-TURNER
OVERDRIVE**
952 You Ain't Seen Nothing Yet

BAD ENGLISH
580 When I See You Smile

BANANARAMA
832 Venus

BANGLES
230 Walk Like An Egyptian
890 Eternal Flame

BARENAKED LADIES
704 One Week

BASIL, Toni
673 Mickey

BAXTER, Les
81 The Poor People Of Paris

BAY CITY ROLLERS
917 Saturday Night

BEACH BOYS, The
465 I Get Around
565 Help Me, Rhonda
844 Good Vibrations
940 Kokomo

BEATLES, The
32 Hey Jude
65 I Want To Hold Your Hand
110 Get Back
152 Can't Buy Me Love
245 Yesterday
344 Hello Goodbye
371 We Can Work It Out
373 I Feel Fine
381 Help!
422 She Loves You
423 Let It Be
520 A Hard Day's Night
624 The Long And Winding Road
632 Paperback Writer
633 Eight Days A Week
708 Come Together
864 All You Need Is Love
930 Love Me Do
938 Ticket To Ride
965 Penny Lane

BEE GEES
46 Night Fever
172 Stayin' Alive
205 How Can You Mend A Broken Heart
252 How Deep Is Your Love
448 Too Much Heaven
459 Tragedy
515 Jive Talkin'
831 You Should Be Dancing
948 Love You Inside Out

BELL, Archie, & The Drells
470 Tighten Up

BELLAMY BROTHERS
833 Let Your Love Flow

BELLE, Regina
674 A Whole New World (Aladdin's
     Theme)
     PEABO BRYSON and REGINA BELLE

BERLIN
815 Take My Breath Away

BERRY, Chuck
614 My Ding-A-Ling

BEYONCÉ
28 Baby Boy
     BEYONCÉ feat. Sean Paul
37 Crazy In Love
     BEYONCÉ (Featuring Jay-Z)

BILK, Mr. Acker
669 Stranger On The Shore

BLACKstreet
156 No Diggity
     BLACKstreet (Featuring Dr. Dre)

BLIGE, Mary J.
73 Family Affair

BLONDIE
94 Call Me
504 Rapture
675 The Tide Is High
798 Heart Of Glass

BLUE SWEDE
811 Hooked On A Feeling

BOLTON, Michael
377 How Am I Supposed To Live Without
     You
703 When A Man Loves A Woman

BONDS, Gary (U.S.)
518 Quarter To Three

BONE THUGS-N-HARMONY
47 Tha Crossroads

BON JOVI
242 Livin' On A Prayer
607 Bad Medicine
754 Blaze Of Glory
     JON BON JOVI
876 You Give Love A Bad Name
895 I'll Be There For You

BOONE, Debby
23 You Light Up My Life

BOONE, Pat
52 Love Letters In The Sand
88 April Love
169 I Almost Lost My Mind
394 Ain't That A Shame
654 Don't Forbid Me
924 Moody River

BOSTON
611 Amanda

BOWIE, David
588 Fame
683 Let's Dance

BOX TOPS, The
235 The Letter

BOYZ II MEN
1 One Sweet Day
     MARIAH CAREY & BOYZ II MEN
4 I'll Make Love To You
7 End of the Road
77 On Bended Knee
672 4 Seasons Of Loneliness

BRANDY
8 The Boy Is Mine
     BRANDY & MONICA
402 Have You Ever?

BRAXTON, Toni
12 Un-Break My Heart
636 You're Makin' Me High

BREAD
687 Make It With You

BROWN, Bobby
546 She Ain't Worth It
     GLENN MEDEIROS Featuring Bobby
     Brown
783 My Prerogative

BROWN, Chris
138 Run It!

BROWN, Sleepy — see OUTKAST

BROWNS, The
203 The Three Bells

BRYSON, Peabo
674 A Whole New World (Aladdin's Theme)
   PEABO BRYSON and REGINA BELLE

B2K
664 Bump, Bump, Bump
   B2K & P. DIDDY

BUCKINGHAMS, The
574 Kind Of A Drag

BYRDS, The
339 Turn! Turn! Turn! (To Everything There Is A Season)
859 Mr. Tambourine Man

C

CAMPBELL, Glen
441 Rhinestone Cowboy
744 Southern Nights

C & C MUSIC FACTORY
443 Gonna Make You Sweat (Everybody Dance Now)

CAPTAIN & TENNILLE
243 Love Will Keep Us Together
648 Do That To Me One More Time

CARA, Irene
87 Flashdance...What A Feeling

CAREY, Mariah
1 One Sweet Day
   MARIAH CAREY & BOYZ II MEN
3 We Belong Together
38 Fantasy
42 Dreamlover
163 Hero
240 Vision Of Love
312 Honey
346 Emotions
347 Love Takes Time
390 Always Be My Baby
501 Heartbreaker
   MARIAH CAREY (Featuring Jay-Z)
503 I'll Be There
506 I Don't Wanna Cry
537 Someday
660 My All
970 Thank God I Found You
   MARIAH With Joe & 98°
993 Shake It Off

CARLISLE, Belinda
872 Heaven Is A Place On Earth

CARNES, Kim
30 Bette Davis Eyes

CARPENTERS
191 (They Long To Be) Close To You
489 Top Of The World
953 Please Mr. Postman

CASSIDY, Shaun
830 Da Doo Ron Ron

CETERA, Peter
587 Glory Of Love
874 The Next Time I Fall
   PETER CETERA w/AMY GRANT

CHAMPS, The
126 Tequila

CHANDLER, Gene
338 Duke Of Earl

CHANNEL, Bruce
336 Hey! Baby

CHAPIN, Harry
915 Cat's In The Cradle

CHARLES, Ray
130 I Can't Stop Loving You
522 Hit The Road Jack
960 Georgia On My Mind

CHEAP TRICK
583 The Flame

CHECKER, Chubby
246 The Twist
322 Pony Time

CHER
162 Believe
458 Gypsys, Tramps & Thieves
502 Half-Breed
922 Dark Lady

CHIC
84 Le Freak
718 Good Times

CHICAGO
410 Hard To Say I'm Sorry
447 If You Leave Me Now
485 Look Away

CHIFFONS, The
222 He's So Fine

CHI-LITES, The
813 Oh Girl

CHINGY
1000 Right Thurr

CHIPMUNKS, The
244 The Chipmunk Song

CHRISTIE, Lou
933 Lightnin' Strikes

CIARA
51 Goodies
   CIARA featuring Petey Pablo
987 1,2 Step
   CIARA featuring Missy Elliott

CLAPTON, Eric
959 I Shot The Sheriff

CLARK, Dave, Five
932 Over And Over

CLARK, Petula
467 Downtown
626 My Love

CLARKSON, Kelly
563 A Moment Like This

CLUB NOUVEAU
613 Lean On Me

COASTERS, The
714 Yakety Yak

COCKER, Joe
350 Up Where We Belong
   JOE COCKER and JENNIFER WARNES

COLLINS, Phil
202 Another Day In Paradise
285 Against All Odds (Take A Look At Me Now)
550 Two Hearts
597 Groovy Kind Of Love
610 One More Night
702 Separate Lives
   PHIL COLLINS and MARILYN MARTIN
893 Sussudio

COLOR ME BADD
542 I Adore Mi Amor
645 All 4 Love

COMMODORES
415 Three Times A Lady
656 Still

COMO, Perry
398 Round And Round
649 Hot Diggity (Dog Ziggity Boom)
662 Catch A Falling Star

CONTI, Bill
761 Gonna Fly Now

COOKE, Sam
261 You Send Me

COOLIO
247 Gangsta's Paradise
   COOLIO featuring L.V.

CORTEZ, Dave "Baby"
810 The Happy Organ

COUGAR, John — see MELLENCAMP

COX, Deborah
980 Nobody's Supposed To Be Here

CRAZY TOWN
484 Butterfly

CREED
638 With Arms Wide Open

CRICKETS — see HOLLY, Buddy

CROCE, Jim
486 Bad, Bad Leroy Brown
557 Time In A Bottle

CROSS, Christopher
267 Arthur's Theme (Best That You Can Do)
816 Sailing

CROW, Sheryl
991 All I Wanna Do

CRYSTALS, The
555 He's A Rebel

CULTURE CLUB
299 Karma Chameleon

CUTTING CREW
602 (I Just) Died In Your Arms

D

DALE & GRACE
559 I'm Leaving It Up To You

DAMIAN, Michael
946 Rock On

DANNY & THE JUNIORS
61 At The Hop

D'ARBY, Terence Trent
869 Wishing Well

DARIN, Bobby
27 Mack The Knife

DAVIS, Mac
305 Baby Don't Get Hooked On Me

DAVIS, Sammy Jr.
349 The Candy Man

DAWN — see ORLANDO, Tony

DAYNE, Taylor
875 Love Will Lead You Back

DEAN, Jimmy
140 Big Bad John

DEE, Joey, & the Starliters
278 Peppermint Twist - Part I

DEE, Kiki
231 Don't Go Breaking My Heart
   ELTON JOHN and KIKI DEE

DEES, Rick, And His Cast Of Idiots
676 Disco Duck (Part I)

DEF LEPPARD
894 Love Bites

DENVER, John
564 Annie's Song
822 Sunshine On My Shoulders
941 Thank God I'm A Country Boy
967 I'm Sorry

175

GILDER, Nick
691 Hot Child In The City

GILMER, Jimmy, & The Fireballs
141 Sugar Shack

GOLDSBORO, Bobby
142 Honey

GORE, Lesley
568 It's My Party

GRACIE, Charlie
507 Butterfly

GRAND FUNK RAILROAD
589 The Loco-Motion
904 We're An American Band

GRANT, Amy
529 Baby Baby
874 The Next Time I Fall
      PETER CETERA w/AMY GRANT

GRANT, Gogi
39 The Wayward Wind

GREEN, Al
713 Let's Stay Together

GREENE, Lorne
860 Ringo

GUESS WHO, The
325 American Woman

GUNS N' ROSES
539 Sweet Child O' Mine

H

HALEY, Bill, And His Comets
35 Rock Around The Clock

HALL, Daryl, & John Oates
176 Maneater
313 Kiss On My List
445 Private Eyes
449 Out Of Touch
592 Rich Girl
661 I Can't Go For That (No Can Do)

HAMILTON, JOE FRANK & REYNOLDS
919 Fallin' In Love

HAMMER, Jan
814 Miami Vice Theme

HANSON
265 MMMBop

HARRISON, George
208 My Sweet Lord
741 Got My Mind Set On You
855 Give Me Love - (Give Me Peace On Earth)

HARRISON, Wilbert
516 Kansas City

HAYES, Isaac
478 Theme From Shaft

HEART
316 Alone
898 These Dreams

HEIGHTS, The
430 How Do You Talk To An Angel

HENLEY, Don — see SMYTH, Patty

HERMAN'S HERMITS
372 Mrs. Brown You've Got A Lovely Daughter
939 I'm Henry VIII, I Am

HI-FIVE
696 I Like The Way (The Kissing Game)

HIGHWAYMEN, The
480 Michael

HILL, Faith
998 Breathe

HILL, Lauryn
414 Doo Wop (That Thing)

HOLLY, Buddy/The Crickets
701 That'll Be The Day

HOLLYWOOD ARGYLES
768 Alley-Oop

HOLMES, Rupert
286 Escape (The Pina Colada Song)

HONEY CONE, The
764 Want Ads

HORNSBY, Bruce, And The Range
740 The Way It Is

HORTON, Johnny
91 The Battle Of New Orleans

HOUSTON, Thelma
732 Don't Leave Me This Way

HOUSTON, Whitney
6 I Will Always Love You
355 Greatest Love Of All
457 I Wanna Dance With Somebody (Who Loves Me)
534 All The Man That I Need
553 Didn't We Almost Have It All
578 How Will I Know
603 Where Do Broken Hearts Go
642 Exhale (Shoop Shoop)
757 I'm Your Baby Tonight
758 So Emotional
786 Saving All My Love For You

HUES CORPORATION, The
957 Rock The Boat

HUMAN LEAGUE, The
263 Don't You Want Me
790 Human

HUNTER, Tab
92 Young Love

HYLAND, Brian
766 Itsy Bitsy Teenie Weenie Yellow Polkadot Bikini

I

IDOL, Billy
913 Mony Mony "Live"

IGLESIAS, Enrique
283 Be With You
579 Bailamos

INGRAM, James
438 Baby, Come To Me
      PATTI AUSTIN (with James Ingram)
782 I Don't Have The Heart

INXS
731 Need You Tonight

J

JACKS, Terry
315 Seasons In The Sun

JACKSON, Janet
43 That's The Way Love Goes
57 All For You
233 Miss You Much
264 Doesn't Really Matter
321 Escapade
393 Again
395 Together Again
601 When I Think Of You
785 Love Will Never Do (Without You)
955 Black Cat

JACKSON, Michael
67 Billie Jean
70 Black Or White
90 Say Say Say
      PAUL McCARTNEY AND MICHAEL JACKSON
210 Rock With You

281 Beat It
552 Man In The Mirror
629 Bad
682 You Are Not Alone
849 Ben
902 The Way You Make Me Feel
914 Don't Stop 'Til You Get Enough
931 I Just Can't Stop Loving You
956 Dirty Diana

JACKSON 5, The
127 I'll Be There
476 ABC
477 The Love You Save
706 I Want You Back

JAMES, Sonny
655 Young Love

JAMES, Tommy, And The Shondells
419 Crimson And Clover
623 Hanky Panky

JAN & DEAN
567 Surf City

JA RULE
83 Ain't It Funny
      JENNIFER LOPEZ featuring Ja Rule
108 I'm Real
      JENNIFER LOPEZ featuring Ja Rule
387 Always On Time
      JA RULE (feat. Ashanti)

JAY-Z
37 Crazy In Love
      BEYONCÉ (Featuring Jay-Z)
501 Heartbreaker
      MARIAH CAREY (Featuring Jay-Z)

JEFFERSON STARSHIP — see STARSHIP

JETT, Joan, & The Blackhearts
63 I Love Rock 'N Roll

JOE
168 Stutter
      JOE (featuring Mystikal)
970 Thank God I Found You
      MARIAH With Joe & 98°

JOEL, Billy
413 It's Still Rock And Roll To Me
496 We Didn't Start The Fire
792 Tell Her About It

JOHN, Elton
5 Candle In The Wind 1997/Something About The Way You Look Tonight
195 That's What Friends Are For
      DIONNE & FRIENDS: Elton John, Gladys Knight and Stevie Wonder
231 Don't Go Breaking My Heart
      ELTON JOHN and KIKI DEE
302 Crocodile Rock
364 Island Girl
446 Philadelphia Freedom
620 Lucy In The Sky With Diamonds
707 Bennie And The Jets
736 Don't Let The Sun Go Down On Me
      GEORGE MICHAEL/ELTON JOHN

JOHN, Robert
690 Sad Eyes

JOPLIN, Janis
517 Me And Bobby McGee

JORDAN, Montell
56 This Is How We Do It

JOURNEY
995 Open Arms

JUVENILE
407 Slow Motion
      JUVENILE Featuring Soulja Slim

K

KAEMPFERT, Bert
289 Wonderland By Night

177

McCARTNEY, Paul/Wings
- 64 Ebony And Ivory
  PAUL McCARTNEY (with Stevie Wonder)
- 90 Say Say Say
  PAUL McCARTNEY AND MICHAEL JACKSON
- 128 Silly Love Songs
- 215 My Love
- 275 Coming Up (Live At Glasgow)
- 513 With A Little Luck
- 823 Band On The Run
- 846 Uncle Albert/Admiral Halsey
- 853 Listen To What The Man Said

McCOO, Marilyn, & Billy Davis, Jr.
- 728 You Don't Have To Be A Star (To Be In My Show)

McCOY, Van
- 834 The Hustle

McCOYS, The
- 856 Hang On Sloopy

McCRAE, George
- 630 Rock Your Baby

McDONALD, Michael
- 351 On My Own
  PATTI LaBELLE AND MICHAEL McDONALD

McFERRIN, Bobby
- 596 Don't Worry Be Happy

McGOVERN, Maureen
- 616 The Morning After

McGUIRE, Barry
- 862 Eve Of Destruction

McGUIRE SISTERS, The
- 183 Sugartime

McKNIGHT, Brian
- 981 Back At One

McLEAN, Don
- 190 American Pie - Parts I & II

MEAT LOAF
- 117 I'd Do Anything For Love (But I Won't Do That)

MECO
- 600 Star Wars Theme/Cantina Band

MEDEIROS, Glenn
- 546 She Ain't Worth It
  GLENN MEDEIROS Featuring Bobby Brown

MEDLEY, Bill
- 873 (I've Had) The Time Of My Life
  BILL MEDLEY AND JENNIFER WARNES

MELANIE
- 293 Brand New Key

MELLENCAMP, John Cougar
- 196 Jack & Diane

MEN AT WORK
- 194 Down Under
- 693 Who Can It Be Now?

MFSB
- 594 TSOP (The Sound Of Philadelphia)
  MFSB featuring The Three Degrees

MICHAEL, George/Wham!
- 214 Faith
- 298 Careless Whisper
  WHAM! Featuring George Michael
- 317 Wake Me Up Before You Go-Go
  WHAM!
- 356 One More Try
- 556 I Knew You Were Waiting (For Me)
  ARETHA FRANKLIN AND GEORGE MICHAEL
- 591 Everything She Wants
  WHAM!
- 605 Father Figure
- 615 Monkey

- 736 Don't Let The Sun Go Down On Me
  GEORGE MICHAEL/ELTON JOHN
- 934 Praying For Time

MIDLER, Bette
- 780 Wind Beneath My Wings

MIKE + THE MECHANICS
- 885 The Living Years

MILLER, Mitch
- 82 The Yellow Rose Of Texas

MILLER, Steve, Band
- 399 Abracadabra
- 737 The Joker
- 943 Rock'n Me

MILLI VANILLI
- 584 Blame It On The Rain
- 586 Girl I'm Gonna Miss You
- 883 Baby Don't Forget My Number

MINDBENDERS — see FONTANA, Wayne

MIRACLES, The
- 435 The Tears Of A Clown
- 865 Love Machine (Part 1)

MR. BIG
- 296 To Be With You

MR. MISTER
- 453 Broken Wings
- 547 Kyrie

MITCHELL, Guy
- 20 Singing The Blues
- 429 Heartaches By The Number

MODUGNO, Domenico
- 139 Nel Blu Dipinto Di Blu (Volaré)

MONICA
- 8 The Boy Is Mine
  BRANDY & MONICA
- 110 The First Night
- 166 Angel Of Mine

MONKEES, The
- 66 I'm A Believer
- 209 Daydream Believer
- 726 Last Train To Clarksville

MURPHY, Walter
- 671 A Fifth Of Beethoven

MURRAY, Anne
- 730 You Needed Me

MYA
- 122 Lady Marmalade
  CHRISTINA AGUILERA, LIL' KIM, MYA and P!NK

MYLES, Alannah
- 533 Black Velvet

MYSTIKAL — see JOE

N

NASH, Johnny
- 232 I Can See Clearly Now

NATE DOGG — see 50 CENT

NELLY
- 17 Dilemma
  NELLY Featuring Kelly Rowland
- 50 Hot In Herre
- 177 Shake Ya Tailfeather
  NELLY/P. DIDDY/MURPHY LEE

NELSON
- 794 (Can't Live Without Your) Love And Affection

NELSON, Ricky
- 420 Poor Little Fool
- 498 Travelin' Man

NEW KIDS ON THE BLOCK
- 369 Step By Step
- 881 I'll Be Loving You (Forever)
- 920 Hangin' Tough

NEWTON-JOHN, Olivia
- 21 Physical
- 211 Magic
- 631 I Honestly Love You
- 698 You're The One That I Want
  JOHN TRAVOLTA AND OLIVIA NEWTON-JOHN
- 850 Have You Never Been Mellow

NEW VAUDEVILLE BAND, The
- 294 Winchester Cathedral

NEXT
- 107 Too Close

NICKELBACK
- 153 How You Remind Me

NILSSON
- 217 Without You

98° — see CAREY, Mariah

NOTORIOUS B.I.G., The
- 319 Hypnotize
- 406 Mo Money Mo Problems
  THE NOTORIOUS B.I.G. Featuring Puff Daddy & Mase

*NSYNC
- 412 It's Gonna Be Me

O

OCEAN, Billy
- 531 Caribbean Queen (No More Love On The Run)
- 544 Get Outta My Dreams, Get Into My Car
- 799 There'll Be Sad Songs (To Make You Cry)

O'CONNOR, Sinéad
- 199 Nothing Compares 2 U

O'DAY, Alan
- 776 Undercover Angel

OHIO PLAYERS
- 686 Love Rollercoaster
- 968 Fire

O'JAYS, The
- 910 Love Train

OLIVIA — see 50 CENT

112 — see PUFF DADDY

ORBISON, Roy
- 324 Oh, Pretty Woman
- 966 Running Scared

ORLANDO, Tony, & Dawn
- 189 Tie A Yellow Ribbon Round The Ole Oak Tree
- 277 Knock Three Times
- 383 He Don't Love You (Like I Love You)

OSMOND, Donny
- 306 Go Away Little Girl

OSMONDS, The
- 148 One Bad Apple

O'SULLIVAN, Gilbert
- 99 Alone Again (Naturally)

OUTKAST
- 25 Hey Ya!
- 635 The Way You Move
  OUTKAST Featuring Sleepy Brown
- 657 Ms. Jackson

P

PABLO, Petey — see CIARA

PAGE, Tommy
- 949 I'll Be Your Everything

PALMER, Robert
- 796 Addicted To Love

PAPER LACE
- 928 The Night Chicago Died

THE SONGS

This section lists, alphabetically, all song titles listed in the Top 1000 ranking. Listed next to each song title is its final ranking in the Top 1000.

A song with more than one charted version is listed once, with the artist's names listed below it in rank order. Songs that have the same title, but are different tunes, are listed separately, with the highest-ranked song listed first.

A

476 **ABC** *Jackson 5*
399 **Abracadabra** *Steve Miller Band*
796 **Addicted To Love** *Robert Palmer*
867 **Africa** *Toto*
505 **Afternoon Delight**
 Starland Vocal Band
393 **Again** *Janet Jackson*
285 **Against All Odds (Take A Look
 At Me Now)** *Phil Collins*
83 **Ain't It Funny** *Jennifer Lopez*
308 **Ain't No Mountain High Enough**
 Diana Ross
394 **Ain't That A Shame** *Pat Boone*
645 **All 4 Love** *Color Me Badd*
257 **All For Love**
 Bryan Adams/Rod Stewart/Sting
57 **All For You** *Janet Jackson*
181 **All I Have** *Jennifer Lopez*
123 **All I Have To Do Is Dream**
 Everly Brothers
991 **All I Wanna Do** *Sheryl Crow*
262 **All My Life** *K-Ci & JoJo*
175 **All Night Long (All Night)**
 Lionel Richie
29 **All Shook Up** *Elvis Presley*
534 **All The Man That I Need**
 Whitney Houston
864 **All You Need Is Love** *Beatles*
768 **Alley-Oop** *Hollywood Argyles*
316 **Alone** *Heart*
99 **Alone Again (Naturally)**
 Gilbert O'Sullivan
797 **Always** *Atlantic Starr*
390 **Always Be My Baby**
 Mariah Carey
387 **Always On Time** *Ja Rule*
611 **Amanda** *Boston*
405 **Amazed** *Lonestar*
190 **American Pie** *Don McLean*
325 **American Woman** *Guess Who*
647 **Angel** *Shaggy*
166 **Angel Of Mine** *Monica*
828 **Angie** *Rolling Stones*
903 **Angie Baby** *Helen Reddy*
564 **Annie's Song** *John Denver*
182 **Another Brick In The Wall**
 Pink Floyd
202 **Another Day In Paradise**
 Phil Collins
255 **Another One Bites The Dust**
 Queen
540 **Anything For You** *Gloria Estefan*
88 **April Love** *Pat Boone*
97 **Aquarius/Let The Sunshine In**
 5th Dimension
101 **Are You Lonesome To-night?**
 Elvis Presley
267 **Arthur's Theme (Best That You
 Can Do)** *Christopher Cross*
61 **At The Hop** *Danny & The Juniors*
582 **At This Moment**
 Billy Vera & The Beaters
157 **Autumn Leaves** *Roger Williams*

B

421 **Babe** *Styx*
529 **Baby Baby** *Amy Grant*
992 **Baby-Baby-Baby** *TLC*
28 **Baby Boy** *Beyoncé*
284 **Baby Come Back** *Player*
438 **Baby, Come To Me**
 Patti Austin (with James Ingram)
883 **Baby Don't Forget My Number**
 Milli Vanilli
305 **Baby Don't Get Hooked On Me**
 Mac Davis
111 **Baby Got Back** *Sir Mix-A-Lot*
870 **Baby, I Love Your Way/Freebird
 Medley (Free Baby)**
 Will To Power
239 **Baby Love** *Supremes*

396 **Baby One More Time**
 Britney Spears
981 **Back At One** *Brian McKnight*
963 **Back In My Arms Again**
 Supremes
629 **Bad** *Michael Jackson*
486 **Bad, Bad Leroy Brown** *Jim Croce*
384 **Bad Blood** *Neil Sedaka*
133 **Bad Girls** *Donna Summer*
607 **Bad Medicine** *Bon Jovi*
579 **Bailamos** *Enrique Iglesias*
996 **Baker Street** *Gerry Rafferty*
150 **Ballad Of The Green Berets**
 SSgt Barry Sadler
823 **Band On The Run**
 Paul McCartney
927 **Batdance** *Prince*
91 **Battle Of New Orleans**
 Johnny Horton
283 **Be With You** *Enrique Iglesias*
281 **Beat It** *Michael Jackson*
197 **Because I Love You (The
 Postman Song)** *Stevie B*
74 **Because You Loved Me**
 Celine Dion
743 **Before The Next Teardrop Falls**
 Freddy Fender
162 **Believe** *Cher*
849 **Ben** *Michael Jackson*
707 **Bennie And The Jets** *Elton John*
644 **Bent** *Matchbox Twenty*
121 **Best Of My Love** *Emotions*
889 **Best Of My Love** *Eagles*
30 **Bette Davis Eyes** *Kim Carnes*
140 **Big Bad John** *Jimmy Dean*
137 **Big Girls Don't Cry** *4 Seasons*
572 **Big Hunk O' Love** *Elvis Presley*
67 **Billie Jean** *Michael Jackson*
678 **Bills, Bills, Bills** *Destiny's Child*
554 **Billy, Don't Be A Hero**
 Bo Donaldson
670 **Bird Dog** *Everly Brothers*
964 **Black & White** *Three Dog Night*
955 **Black Cat** *Janet Jackson*
70 **Black Or White** *Michael Jackson*
533 **Black Velvet** *Alannah Myles*
835 **Black Water** *Doobie Brothers*
584 **Blame It On The Rain** *Milli Vanilli*
754 **Blaze Of Glory** *Jon Bon Jovi*
745 **Blinded By The Light**
 Manfred Mann's Earth Band
340 **Blue Moon** *Marcels*
335 **Blue Velvet** *Bobby Vinton*
788 **Boogie Fever** *Sylvers*
268 **Boogie Oogie Oogie**
 Taste Of Honey
609 **Bootylicious** *Destiny's Child*
8 **Boy Is Mine** *Brandy & Monica*
293 **Brand New Key** *Melanie*
685 **Brandy (You're A Fine Girl)**
 Looking Glass
560 **Breaking Up Is Hard To Do**
 Neil Sedaka
998 **Breathe** *Faith Hill*
104 **Bridge Over Troubled Water**
 Simon & Garfunkel
453 **Broken Wings** *Mr. Mister*
497 **Brother Louie** *Stories*
521 **Brown Sugar** *Rolling Stones*
664 **Bump, Bump, Bump**
 B2K & P. Diddy
178 **Bump N' Grind** *R. Kelly*
36 **Burn** *Usher*
292 **Butterfly**
 Andy Williams
507 *Charlie Gracie*
484 **Butterfly** *Crazy Town*

C

462 **Calcutta** *Lawrence Welk*
94 **Call Me** *Blondie*
152 **Can't Buy Me Love** *Beatles*
320 **Can't Fight This Feeling**
 REO Speedwagon

972 **Can't Get Enough Of Your Love,
 Babe** *Barry White*
54 **Can't Help Falling In Love** *UB40*
794 **(Can't Live Without You) Love
 And Affection** *Nelson*
79 **Can't Nobody Hold Me Down**
 Puff Daddy
5 **Candle In The Wind 1997**
 Elton John
349 **Candy Man** *Sammy Davis, Jr.*
31 **Candy Shop** *50 Cent*
715 **Car Wash** *Rose Royce*
298 **Careless Whisper** *Wham!*
531 **Caribbean Queen (No More Love
 On The Run)** *Billy Ocean*
915 **Cat's In The Cradle** *Harry Chapin*
662 **Catch A Falling Star** *Perry Como*
145 **Cathy's Clown** *Everly Brothers*
527 **Celebration** *Kool & The Gang*
93 **Centerfold** *J. Geils Band*
650 **Chances Are** *Johnny Mathis*
370 **Chapel Of Love** *Dixie Cups*
709 **Chariots Of Fire** *Vangelis*
380 **Cherish** *Association*
244 **Chipmunk Song** *Chipmunks*
775 **Close To You** *Maxi Priest*
742 **Cold Hearted** *Paula Abdul*
877 **Come On Eileen**
 Dexys Midnight Runners
229 **Come On Over Baby (all I want is
 you)** *Christina Aguilera*
472 **Come See About Me** *Supremes*
237 **Come Softly To Me** *Fleetwoods*
708 **Come Together** *Beatles*
545 **Coming Out Of The Dark**
 Gloria Estefan
275 **Coming Up (Live At Glasgow)**
 Paul McCartney
401 **Confessions Part II** *Usher*
851 **Convoy** *C.W. McCall*
590 **Could've Been** *Tiffany*
812 **Cracklin' Rosie** *Neil Diamond*
716 **Crazy For You** *Madonna*
37 **Crazy In Love** *Beyoncé*
187 **Crazy Little Thing Called Love**
 Queen
530 **Cream** *Prince*
154 **Creep** *TLC*
419 **Crimson And Clover**
 Tommy James & The Shondells
302 **Crocodile Rock** *Elton John*
47 **Crossroads, Tha**
 Bone Thugs-N-Harmony

D

830 **Da Doo Ron Ron** *Shaun Cassidy*
185 **Da Ya Think I'm Sexy?**
 Rod Stewart
739 **Dancing Queen** *Abba*
922 **Dark Lady** *Cher*
209 **Daydream Believer** *Monkees*
378 **December, 1963 (Oh, What a
 Night)** *Four Seasons*
842 **Deep Purple**
 Nino Tempo & April Stevens
756 **Delta Dawn** *Helen Reddy*
658 **Diana** *Paul Anka*
553 **Didn't We Almost Have It All**
 Whitney Houston
17 **Dilemma** *Nelly*
956 **Dirty Diana** *Michael Jackson*
676 **Disco Duck** *Rick Dees*
234 **Disco Lady** *Johnnie Taylor*
219 **Dizzy** *Tommy Roe*
648 **Do That To Me One More Time**
 Captain & Tennille
479 **Do Wah Diddy Diddy**
 Manfred Mann
264 **Doesn't Really Matter**
 Janet Jackson
225 **Dominique** *Singing Nun*
131 **Don't** *Elvis Presley*
13 **Don't Be Cruel** *Elvis Presley*

185

Artists with the Most
Top 1000 Ranked Hits

# of Hits		
20	1.	The Beatles
18	2.	Elvis Presley
17	3.	Mariah Carey
13	4.	Michael Jackson
12	5.	Madonna
12	6.	The Supremes
11	7.	Whitney Houston
10	8.	Elton John
10	9.	Janet Jackson
10	10.	George Michael/Wham!
10	11.	Stevie Wonder
9	12.	Paul McCartney/Wings
9	13.	Bee Gees
8	14.	Usher
8	15.	The Rolling Stones
7	16.	Phil Collins
6	17.	Pat Boone
6	18.	Puff Daddy
6	19.	Diana Ross
6	20.	Daryl Hall & John Oates
6	21.	Paula Abdul
5	22.	Boyz II Men
5	23.	Lionel Richie
5	24.	The 4 Seasons
5	25.	TLC
5	26.	Barbra Streisand
5	27.	Celine Dion
5	28.	Olivia Newton-John
5	29.	Destiny's Child
5	30.	Prince
5	31.	Bon Jovi
5	32.	KC & The Sunshine Band
5	33.	Eagles

BREAKDOWN BY YEAR

Total records making the Top 1000 year-by-year:

YR	TOP 1000		YR	TOP 1000
55	8		60	19
56	16		61	21
57	21		62	19
58	23		63	21
59	15		64	23
			65	25
Total	**83** (8.3%)		66	27
			67	18
			68	15
			69	16
			Total	**204** (20.4%)

YR	TOP 1000		YR	TOP 1000
70	21		80	16
71	18		81	17
72	21		82	16
73	27		83	16
74	35		84	19
75	35		85	26
76	26		86	30
77	28		87	29
78	20		88	32
79	23		89	32
Total	**254** (25.4%)		**Total**	**233** (23.3%)

YR	TOP 1000		YR	TOP 1000
90	25		00	18
91	27		01	15
92	15		02	9
93	11		03	12
94	10		04	12
95	11		05	9
96	10			
97	10		**Total**	**75** (7.5%)
98	17			
99	15			
Total	**151** (15.1%)			

THOUSANDS MORE
CHARTED HITS...
AT YOUR FINGERTIPS!

Now dig deeper and wider into charted music with Joel Whitburn's Record Research Collection — the only books that get right to the bottom of Billboard's major charts. With complete, accurate data on every charted recording. And comprehensive facts and stats on charted music's biggest hits and artists.

Joel Whitburn and his Record Researchers have been highlighting the hits…archiving the artists…and tracking the trends longer, deeper and in more definitive detail than anyone else anywhere. There's no one better to bring you all the facts on all the hits on all the charts beyond The Top 1000 — with an unerring accuracy you can count on!

For detailed book descriptions, complete sample pages and shipping information, visit us at: **recordresearch.com**. Or call **800-827-9810**.

Joel Whitburn's
TOP POP SINGLES

Our all-time bestseller has never been a more useful, convenient and valuable addition to your music library! From vinyl 45s to CD singles to album tracks, here—and only here—are the more than 25,000 titles and 6,000 artists that appeared on Billboard's Pop music charts from 1955-2002…all arranged by artist for fast, easy reference! With key facts, hot hits and informative features highlighted in red. Bigger, beefier artist bios. Expanded, more accurate title notes. And updated record and CD pricing.

1,024 pages
Size: 7" x 9"
Hardcover

$44⁹⁵

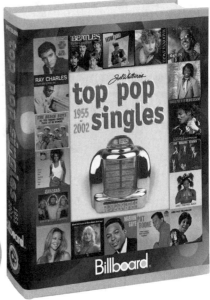

Joel Whitburn's
THE BILLBOARD® ALBUMS
6ᵀᴴ EDITION

Over 25,000 charted Billboard albums. Over 270,000 Billboard album tracks. Over 6,000 Billboard album artists. All here—and only here—in the only book of its kind anywhere. This 50-year, artist-by-artist history of the rock era includes every album that made "The Billboard 200®" chart from 1956 through December 31, 2005. It's packed with essential chart data…updated artist bios and title notes…and, for each artist, a master A-Z index of all tracks from all of their albums!

Over 1,400 pages
Size: 7" x 9"
Hardcover

$79⁹⁵

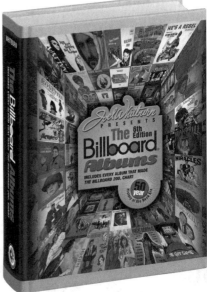

Joel Whitburn's
POP ANNUAL

Count 'em down and download 'em to your digital player—45 year-by-year rankings, in numerical order according to the highest chart position reached, of the 23,070 singles that peaked on Billboard's Pop singles charts from 1955-1999. Includes comprehensive, essential chart data and more—all conveniently arranged for fast, easy reference. A must for every music enthusiast's bookshelf and the perfect companion to *Top Pop Singles*!

912 pages
Size: 7" x 9"

$44⁹⁵
Softcover

$54⁹⁵
Hardcover

Joel Whitburn's
POP HITS
SINGLES &
ALBUMS
1940-1954

The big bands. The classic crooners. The classy female vocalists. The smooth vocal groups. The dynamic duos. Here's the complete history of pre-Rock Pop in four big books in one! An artist-by-artist singles anthology; a year-by-year ranking of classic Pop hits; the complete story of early Pop albums; plus the weekly "Best Sellers" Top 10 singles charts of 1940-1954.

576 pages
Size: 7" x 9"
Hardcover

$39⁹⁵

Joel Whitburn's
TOP R&B/HIP-HOP SINGLES

From R&B's early pioneers...to today's hottest Hip-Hop stars! Over 4,400 artists and nearly 20,000 song titles from Billboard's Rhythm & Blues/Soul/Black/Hip-Hop Singles charts from 1942-2004—all arranged by artist! With complete R&B chart data...R&B record and artist info... and much more.

816 pages
Size: 7" x 9"
Hardcover

$59⁹⁵

Joel Whitburn's
TOP R&B ALBUMS

Covers every artist and album to appear on Billboard's "Top R&B Albums" chart from 1965-1998, with complete chart info... features highlighting each artist's hit albums and hot chart eras...complete track listings for Top 10 albums...and more!

360 pages
Size: 7" x 9"
Hardcover

$29⁹⁵

BILLBOARD "HOT 100" SINGLES CHART BOOKS

Straight from the pages of Billboard -- each decade's "Hot 100" and Pop singles music charts, with every weekly chart reproduced in black and white at about 70% of its original size. **Various page lengths. Sizes: 50's –70's, 90's– 9" x 12", 80's– 8¹/₂" x 11". Hardcover.**

$59 ⁹⁵ $79 ⁹⁵ $79 ⁹⁵ $79 ⁹⁵ $79 ⁹⁵

**Billboard Pop Charts
1955-1959**

**Billboard Hot 100
Charts The Sixties**

**Billboard Hot 100
Charts The Seventies**

**Billboard Hot 100
Charts The Eighties**

**Billboard Hot 100
Charts The Nineties**

Visit www.recordresearch.com for book descriptions, sample pages and shipping terms.

Joel Whitburn's
TOP COUNTRY SONGS

An artist-by-artist listing of all charted Country hits, covering the complete chart careers of legendary Country greats and introducing fresh Country voices, with the chart data lowdown and songwriter(s) for every "Country" single from 1944-2005!

624 pages
Size: 7" x 9"
Hardcover

$59.95

Joel Whitburn's
COUNTRY ANNUAL

54 complete, year-by-year rankings of over 16,000 records that peaked on Billboard's Country singles charts from 1944-1997, with each song ranked according to its highest chart position.

704 pages
Size: 7" x 9"
Hardcover

$34.95

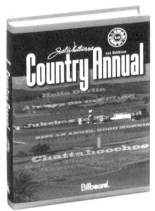

Joel Whitburn's
TOP COUNTRY ALBUMS

The album chart histories of Country's greats—an artist-by-artist chronicle of every album to appear on Billboard's "Top Country Albums" chart from 1964-1997, with complete chart data, Top 10 album track listings, and more.

304 pages
Size: 7" x 9"
Hardcover

$29.95

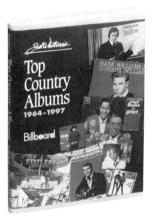

BILLBOARD MUSIC YEARBOOKS

Each Yearbook is a comprehensive annual recap of each year's music, in complete artist-by-artist sections covering Billboard's major singles and albums charts. With complete chart data on every single, track and album that debuted during the year...plus artist biographical info, Time Capsules, entertainment obituaries and more!

Over 200 pages each
Size: 6" x 9" Softcover

80's
$14⁹⁵
each

90's
$19⁹⁵
each

00's
$24⁹⁵
each

ROCK TRACKS

Billboard's two greatest Rock charts—now covered individually in this one book! A total of 22 years of every track and every artist that ever hit Billboard's "Mainstream Rock Tracks" and "Modern Rock Tracks" charts, with comprehensive data on every track from 1981-2002!

336 pages
Size: 7" x 9"
Hardcover

$29⁹⁵

CHRISTMAS IN THE CHARTS

Charted holiday classics cover to cover—a jolly, joyous celebration of America's favorite holiday music from 1920-2004! This complete history of every charted Christmas single and album is drawn from a diversity of Billboard charts and music genres. Arranged by artist, with full chart data and all the trimmings for every Christmas hit!

272 pages
Size: 7" x 9"
Softcover

$29⁹⁵

HOT DANCE/DISCO

Lists every artist and hit to appear on Billboard's national "Dance/Disco Club Play" chart from 1974-2003. All charted titles, album cuts—even complete albums that made the Dance chart in their entirety. Loaded with basic chart facts...intriguing Info on artists and recordings...Top Artists' pix...plus much more!

368 pages
Size: 7" x 9"
Hardcover

$39⁹⁵

Visit www.recordresearch.com for book descriptions, sample pages and shipping terms.

TOP ADULT CONTEMPORARY

The definitive work on the softer side of Pop music—an artist-by-artist compilation listing the nearly 8,000 singles and over 1,900 artists that appeared on Billboard's "Easy Listening" and "Hot Adult Contemporary" singles charts from 1961-2001.

352 pages   Size: 7" x 9"   Hardcover

 **$29⁹⁵**

BILLBOARD TOP 10 SINGLES CHARTS

Includes every weekly Top 10 chart from rock and roll's formative years on Billboard's "Best Sellers" charts (1955-1958), followed by weekly Top 10's drawn from the "Hot 100" (1958-2000).

712 pages   Size: 6" x 9"   Hardcover

 $34⁹⁵

BILLBOARD TOP 10 ALBUM CHARTS

More than 1800 individual Top 10 charts from over 35 years of weekly Billboard Top Album charts, beginning with the August 17, 1963 "Top LP's" chart right through "The Billboard 200" of December 26, 1998.

536 pages   Size: 6" x 9"   Hardcover

 $34⁹⁵

#1 POP PIX

Picture this: 1,045 full-color photos of picture sleeves, sheet music covers or Billboard ads representing every #1 Pop hit from Billboard's Pop/Hot 100 charts, with selected chart data, from 1953-2003.

112 pages   Size: 6" x 9"   Softcover

 $14⁹⁵

#1 ALBUM PIX

1,651 full-color photos—in three separate sections—of album covers of every #1 Pop, Country & R&B album in Billboard chart history, with selected chart data, from 1945-2004.

176 pages   Size: 6" x 9"   Softcover

 $14⁹⁵

BUBBLING UNDER THE BILLBOARD HOT 100

Bursting with over 6,100 titles by more than 3,500 artists who appeared on Billboard's "Bubbling Under" chart—long the home to regional hits that lacked the sales and airplay to hit the Hot 100. Includes recordings by legendary artists before they hit the mainstream...rock's top stars...famous non-music celebrities...and classic one-shot "Bubbling"-only artists in this comprehensive chronology from 1959-2004.

352 pages   Size: 7" x 9"   Hardcover

$39⁹⁵

A CENTURY OF POP MUSIC 1900-1999

100 rankings of the 40 biggest hits of each year of the past century, based on America's weekly popular record charts— with complete chart data on every hit!

256 pages   Size: 7" x 9"   Softcover

$14⁹⁵

POP MEMORIES 1890-1954

An artist-by-artist account of the 65 formative years of recorded popular music—over 1,600 artists and 12,000 recordings in all—with data from popular music charts, surveys and listings.

660 pages   Size: 6" x 9"   Hardcover

$44⁹⁵

ALBUM CUTS

Nearly 1/4 million cuts from over 22,000 Pop albums that charted from 1955-2001, listed alphabetically, with the artist's name and chart debut year for each cut. The perfect partner for *Songs & Artists 2006*!

720 pages   Size: 7" x 9"   Hardcover

$24⁹⁵

BILLBOARD POP ALBUM CHARTS 1965-1969

A complete collection of actual reproductions of every weekly Billboard "Top LP's" Pop albums chart from January 2, 1965 through December 27, 1969— each shown in its entirety, in black-and-white, at about 70% of original size.

496 pages   Size: 9" x 12"   Hardcover

$49⁹⁵

SONGS & ARTISTS 2006

Turn your iPod into myPod with the must-have personal playlists from the undisputed experts on recorded music! This perfect companion handbook for your portable MP3 player lists over 14,000 significant songs and essential hits of the past half century. Here are comprehensive playlists for each artist of each half decade's significant songs plus special interest playlists for your favorite activities and musical genres.

288 pages   Size: 6" x 9"   Softcover

$9⁹⁵

BILLBOARD #1s

See in seconds which record held the top spot each and every week for 42 years (1950-1991) on Billboard's Pop, R&B and Country singles and albums charts and Adult Contemporary singles chart.

336 pages   Size: 7" x 9"   Softcover

$19⁹⁵

Visit www.recordresearch.com for book descriptions, sample pages and shipping terms.